"Every Christian I know gets stu
journey doing something they don't want to do. In this book, JP not only shows you the way out but also presents a biblical and practical path to freedom that only Jesus can offer."

Jennie Allen, *New York Times* bestselling author of *Find Your People*; founder and visionary of IF: Gathering

"The question, *Why do I do what I don't want to do?* is a point of tension right from the Scriptures. It is one we all ask, or should be asking. In this adventure of a book, JP illuminates common vices that are prone to find us. Better yet, he teaches us how to stop the drift toward depravities and turn to lifegiving virtues that heal our souls. His personal approach, along with the use of his own testimony, demonstrates that victory is possible and showcases God's limitless grace."

Kyle Idleman, senior pastor of Southeast Christian; bestselling author of *Not a Fan* and *One at a Time*

"For over twenty years now I have counseled with, prayed with, and cried with Christians who feel stuck in patterns of sin they can't seem to break out of. They love Jesus, read the Bible, and many belong to a small group, yet they can't seem to walk in the victory they know is theirs in Jesus. Jonathan Pokluda has served us well in this book. He masterfully shows how the church has historically defined and diagnosed this battle—and a way forward through its more modern iterations. If you feel stuck, this is the book for you."

Matt Chandler, lead pastor of The Village Church

"JP uses years of hard-earned wisdom to build this message for the masses. Whether you're seventeen or seventy, you'll be challenged and encouraged with truth. But JP knows you can't make these changes on your own—that's why he goes to great lengths to anchor every chapter in Scripture and the hope of the gospel. He repeatedly points us toward the God who equips us for the growth we all desire as he conforms us to his image."

Tara-Leigh Cobble, author and host of
The Bible Recap book and podcast

"Doctors told me I would die if I didn't quit drinking. I knew they were right; the problem was I didn't know how to stop. We all have a desire to do things that are harmful to us. We often choose to do the harmful things rather than pursue a virtuous life that honors God. But here I am about twenty years sober, and I can testify that what you'll read in this book—or rather Who—is your ancient, well-worn path to not doing what you don't want to do."

John Elmore, author of *Freedom Starts Today*; teaching
pastor of Watermark Community Church, Dallas, Texas

"Inside this book JP gives words and a voice to all the things that are sometimes too hard for us to say, mainly concerning how we conduct our lives on this side of eternity. There is no self-help book that can align your life with the will of God and the purpose he has for you. JP's intentionality to make this clear sets this book apart from any others. JP understands that without God's intervention we cannot live set-apart lives where we maximize our purpose and potential."

Christian Huff & Sadie Robertson Huff,
founder of *4:8 Men* podcast; author, speaker,
and founder of Live Original

"We all need a bold friend; someone who loves us enough to challenge us, confront us, and call us to a better way. Jonathan Pokluda is that friend. He perfectly mixes I've-been-there humility with let's-get-real honesty. Saturated with Scripture, *Why Do I Do What I Don't Want to Do?* provides timeless answers to present problems without serving up a side dish of shame. If you find yourself caught in the cycle of bad habits, let your friend JP help you release your grip on destructive patterns and embrace a new, beautiful way of living."

Ben Stuart, pastor of Passion City Church DC; author of *Single, Dating, Engaged, Married* and *Rest & War*

"If you want to experience freedom from the self-destructive tendencies, temptations, and traps in your life, this book is for you. JP lays out biblical truth in ways that are compelling, raw, and practical. This book provides guidance toward experiencing more of the life you were made for and how to get there."

David Marvin, director of The Porch at Watermark Church; bestselling author of *We're All Freaking Out (and Why We Don't Need To)*

"JP has written a transformative and highly convicting book. If you are a Christian who wants to grow and get a taste of much-needed humble pie, do yourself a favor and read this. I am so grateful for leaders like JP who are not afraid to say things for the sake of the kingdom."

Kait Warman, bestselling author; dating coach; founder of Heart of Dating

"JP delivers again. This book is power-packed with both inspiration and practical takeaways that will elevate your influence and impact as a follower of Jesus by helping you avoid the traps of vices and find life in virtue. Read this book!"

Brad Lomenick, former president of Catalyst; author of
H3 Leadership and *The Catalyst Leader*

"The wonder of the gospel is that it changes our identity in a moment, then proceeds to change our activity over a lifetime. When the Spirit begins to remove ungodly characteristics from our life, our great need is that he'd replace them with godly ones. That is why this book, *Why Do I Do What I Don't Want to Do?*, by my friend Jonathan Pokluda is so relevant and helpful. I always recommend anything he writes, but I believe this book is especially practical for every single person navigating what it means to be a follower of Jesus."

Shane Pruitt, national next gen director of North American Mission Board (NAMB); author of
9 Common Lies Christians Believe

"This book wrestles with the question the apostle Paul asked nearly two thousand years go. I'm excited for many others to benefit from my friend's wisdom and the biblical answers he offers for the many struggles we face today. As you turn the pages you will find not only freedom from deadly vices but the way to a virtuous life in Jesus."

Clay Scroggins, author of *How to Lead When You're Not in Charge*

"*Why Do I Do What I Don't Want To Do?* is radically shaking up parts of me I didn't realize needed to be addressed. When I read JP's words, 'If your motive is to do something for the appearance of being holy, you have missed the point completely and are grieving the heart of God'—Ouch! This book packs a heavy punch of truth that will hit you deeply where you need it most. JP is a voice I trust and love. His tone is eloquently gracious, but at the same time, be ready to be challenged and changed."

Rashawn Copeland, founder of Blessed Media; author of *Start Where You Are*

"There are books that give you information and there are books that give you real-life wisdom. This book is the latter— filled with practical and pastoral guidance for how to become the person God created you to be."

Mike Kelsey, lead pastor of preaching and culture, McLean Bible Church

"With every page turned, I experienced these two primary emotions: a holy conviction and a renewed hope. JP has a way with telling stories and unpacking the Bible that both excavates deep within your soul and empowers you with new-found freedom. This book is going to help set a lot of people free!"

Steve Carter, pastor; author of *The Thing Beneath the Thing*

**WHY
DO I DO
WHAT
I DON'T
WANT
TO DO?**

WHY DO I DO WHAT I DON'T WANT TO DO?

REPLACE DEADLY VICES *with* LIFE-GIVING VIRTUES

JONATHAN "JP" POKLUDA
WITH JON GREEN

BakerBooks
a division of Baker Publishing Group
Grand Rapids, Michigan

Published by Baker Books
a division of Baker Publishing Group
PO Box 6287, Grand Rapids, MI 49516-6287
www.bakerbooks.com

Printed in the United States of America

Library of Congress Cataloging-in-Publication Data
Names: Pokluda, Jonathan, 1980– author.
Title: Why do I do what I don't want to do? : replace deadly vices with life-giving virtues / Jonathan "JP" Pokluda with Jon Green.
Description: Grand Rapids, MI : Baker Books, a division of Baker Publishing Group, [2023] | Includes bibliographical references.
Identifiers: LCCN 2022031064 | ISBN 9780801094965 (paperback) | ISBN 9781540903068 (casebound) | ISBN 9781493439485 (ebook)
Subjects: LCSH: Habit breaking—Religious aspects—Christianity. | Virtues. | Vices.
Classification: LCC BV4598.7 .P65 2023 | DDC 152.3/3—dc23/eng/20220829
LC record available at https://lccn.loc.gov/2022031064

The author is represented by the literary agency of The Gates Group Literary Agency.

23   24   25   26   27   28   29   7   6   5

To my dad.

Thank you for the grace you showed me
and the wisdom you taught me. I miss you.

To my mom.

The world may never know how special you are,
but I know. Thank you for showing me The Way.

CONTENTS

INTRODUCTION

We cannot stop a bad habit. We can only replace it with a good one. I become more and more convinced of that reality. We are creatures of habit, and so much of life is making sure we're building healthy ones. To be completely honest with you (which I intend to be for the entirety of this work), I really wrestled with what to title this book. There were no less than fifty different titles we tried out along the way. The last thing I wanted was for it to sound like another self-help book. Your local bookstore (and even the Christian section of that bookstore) is already full of those. You see, I am not trying to help people be smarter sinners.

It is one of my core beliefs that everyone lives forever somewhere—either in heaven or in hell. My goal is to help other Christians, other believers in Jesus, live the righteous lives Jesus desires for us. The only way that will happen is by living fully dependent on the Holy Spirit *and* by doing the things Jesus calls us to do in this life as we pursue holiness. In fact, 1 Peter 1:15 instructs us to be holy in *all* that we do.

But how do we do that? I don't know about you, but that seems like an impossibly high bar to me.

If you have ever parented a toddler (or spent any time around one, for that matter), it does not take long to figure out that toddlers lack something called "impulse control." Their brains aren't fully developed enough to process all of the pros and cons of the decisions they make, so instead they just do whatever feels good or fun in the moment.

One day, when my son Weston was three years old, we were sitting at our dining room table enjoying a meal as a family. In front of him, sitting on his placemat, was a blue cup full of milk. I watched him from across the table as he picked it up and appeared to examine it closely. On the cup was a superhero, so it wasn't too out of the ordinary for him to be looking at his cup so intently at his age. But then he did do something rather strange: he rotated his wrist until the cup was upside down and the milk poured out all over the table.

I jumped up from my seat and said, "Weston, what are you doing?" He remained speechless as the milk poured into his lap like a waterfall from the table. "Why did you do that?" I asked again. He responded with the three most profound words that could come out of a three-year-old's mouth: "I don't know."

"Weston, why did you do that?" I persisted, just hoping I would get some kind of answer that would shine a light on his thought process. And again, he said, "I don't know."

The truth is, while impulse control eventually kicks in, we never quite grow out of that phase of doing the things we know we shouldn't. As I look back on that silly moment at the table and examine my own life through my young adult years into my middle-aged years, I resonate with Weston.

There are many things I've done that I didn't really want to do, but I still did them. Not in a resilient, "do hard things" kind of way but in a rebellious, "I know this isn't good for me, but I'm going to do it anyway" kind of way. And, like Weston, I'm not sure why.

In his letter to the church at Rome (his theological masterpiece), the apostle Paul sums up this internal conflict we all feel at times as believers in Jesus:

> I do not understand what I do. For what I want to do I do not do, but what I hate I do. And if I do what I do not want to do, I agree that the law is good. As it is, it is no longer I myself who do it, but it is sin living in me. For I know that good itself does not dwell in me, that is, in my sinful nature. For I have the desire to do what is good, but I cannot carry it out. For I do not do the good I want to do, but the evil I do not want to do—this I keep on doing. (Rom. 7:15–19)

We are the same way! We want to pursue what is pure, true, righteous, and holy, but for some reason . . . we don't. We do things that pull us away from Jesus. We run toward momentary pleasure or temporal satisfaction. We don't quite know why we do the things we don't want to do.

There are countless times I have looked at something with a lustful intent, even though everything in me knows I shouldn't. I have responded in anger to people instead of showing them the same grace I have been shown. I have felt entitled to purchases I want because I think they will fill some void I feel, even though it never quite scratches the itch. Why do I do this? Why do I do what I don't want to do? And what should I do instead?

Vices & Virtues

If I have learned anything from both my own life and the thousands of individual case studies I have seen up close as a pastor over the past two decades, there are two lessons that stick out the most. One, sin (most often) subtly creeps into our lives. Two, while we love quick fixes, pursuing holiness is a lifelong pursuit full of micro-decisions along the way.

Throughout the pages of this book, we will look at ten different sins (or vices) that seem to trip us up, year after year, generation after generation. With each one of these sins, we will find it can creep into our lives gradually. No one aspires to be consumed by greed or lust, for example. Your heart just often drifts there over time. If you are not careful and on guard, any one of these ten could be the thing that takes you out. At first glance, you may not even feel like it is something you struggle with, but as you press into each chapter and examine your own heart, you may find ways you have been cohabiting with that vice for years without even realizing it.

Along with each sin, there is a corresponding solution (or virtue) to the problem. For example, the solution to the sin of pride is to practice humility. The solution to the sin of anger is to practice forgiveness. We will examine the pages of Scripture to see how to respond in the most God-honoring way we can to each one of these sins that could trip us up.

In his book *A Long Obedience in the Same Direction*, Eugene Peterson says this:

> There is a great market for religious experience in our world; there is little enthusiasm for the patient acquisition of virtue, little inclination to sign up for a long apprenticeship in what earlier generations of Christians called holiness.[1]

His point is simple. We love to experience or feel things, but the day-to-day grind of fleeing sin and pursuing holiness is much more difficult. But just because it is difficult does not mean that it isn't right. This daily commitment to pursuing the things of Jesus is what it means to be a disciple—a follower of Christ. And here is the best part: you can do this.

Change Is Possible

Almost two thousand years ago, the apostle Paul told the church in Rome, "Do not conform to the pattern of this world, *but be transformed by the renewing of your mind.* Then you will be able to test and approve what God's will is—his good, pleasing and perfect will" (Rom. 12:2, emphasis added). At first glance, that sounds great in theory, but is it even possible to renew your mind? To put it simply: yes.

Over the past few decades, scientists have learned that you can, in fact, change (or *renew*) your mind. For centuries, the commonly held assumption among scientists and psychiatrists was that beyond the formative years of childhood and adolescence, the brain was done developing and no longer changeable.

But what they have discovered more recently is something called *neuroplasticity* (*neuro* meaning "of the brain" and *plasticity* meaning that it can change because it is malleable and moldable). This is the idea that if you take your thoughts captive—or if you stop a particular activity and replace it with another activity or thought pattern—that pathway in the brain atrophies and a new pathway is learned.

You create new neurological pathways when you replace these old, bad, destructive, or unhealthy habits and thinking patterns with newer, true, constructive, and healthier ones. How about that? Thousands of years ago, Paul knew what he was talking about! Renewing your mind might be difficult, but it has a promise attached to it: if you do it, you will know God's will.

My prayer for this book is that, as you read about the vices and virtues described in the pages ahead, the Holy Spirit will show where you have given the enemy (Satan) a foothold into your life and that, by looking to God's Word, you will renew your mind as you pursue the life Jesus has called you to. Remember: the only way to conquer a bad habit is to replace it with a better one.

PART 1

THE ANCIENT BATTLES

I loved going to the beach when I was young. One of the perks of growing up in South Texas was that the beach was only a short road trip away, so our family made the trip often. Port Aransas was our go-to family spot. I know, I know; the Texas coast isn't Hawaii, but as a kid you don't really think about that.

I remember one specific trip when I was in elementary school. After parking our car, my mom set up an umbrella, a couple chairs, and our towels. She was nervous to let me swim by myself, so she made me promise to stay where she could see me the entire time.

About a half hour later, I looked up and my mom was gone. I didn't see our umbrella or chairs anywhere. I swam to shore and noticed our car wasn't there either. After all that fuss of "stay where I can see you," she went off and left me?! I wasn't sure what to do, so I started to walk down the beach in search of someone who would give me a couple of quarters for the pay phone. It was then I realized that I was in another area of the beach. I had evidently drifted farther and farther away from my mom. As I walked down the beach, opposite the current, I eventually found her in the same spot.

Sometimes it feels like God is far from us. Often that is because our sin has carried us away. It has distracted us from intimacy with him and turned our attention to the things of this world. All believers wish we could get to some place in our walk with Jesus where we're no longer at risk of drifting. We wish we could shift into cruise control. There is, however, no cruise control in Christianity. To stay near to God, we will have to actively swim exhaustively against the current.

An Ever-Changing List

In the fourth century, a monk named Evagrius Ponticus put pen to paper and decided to sort common temptations into eight different categories, referring to them as "the eight evil thoughts." At the time, he wasn't writing to all Christians—he was just trying to help out some of his fellow monks by explaining how these eight thought patterns could distract them from their ultimate purpose (devotion to Jesus).[1] A couple hundred years later, Pope Gregory I modified the list, shrinking it from eight to seven (saying that pride was the overarching vice). Several centuries after that, Thomas Aquinas took the list and modified it again.

What we are doing in this book is simply taking an idea that has been passed down for almost 1,700 years and tweaking the list again, taking some items from the original list that continue to plague Christians and adding a few modern-day struggles that need to be talked about today. This book is split up into two parts: the ancient battles and the modern wars.

While the world is constantly changing and culture is constantly shifting, these are the five classic sins (or vices) and their corresponding virtues that we will address in Part 1:

- Pride & Humility
- Anger & Forgiveness
- Greed & Generosity
- Apathy & Diligence
- Lust & Self-Control

These sins never appear grouped together in Scripture. Jesus did not rattle off this list in order of significance when he was preaching the Sermon on the Mount. The idea is simple, though: falling prey to these sins, however significant or insignificant they may seem on the surface, will eat away at your soul. Unfortunately, you can take my word for it; I am an expert in sin. I didn't come to faith in Jesus until I was in my twenties, and I had plenty of time to experience each one of these five sins in full. Take it from me: every topic we address in this book will rob you of the life you are capable of living.

Depending on your knowledge of the early church fathers or your church upbringing, you may notice a couple sins from the original "seven deadly sins" list are missing. Gluttony and envy weren't left out because I think they are great ideas (they are not) or because I think they do not matter. Both of those are extremely harmful as well. Gluttony, or overindulgence, ultimately comes down to us *really* wanting something (and using it to numb whatever pain we might be feeling). In this day and age, we do that in a lot of different ways, from how we spend our money to overeating to watching porn to drinking too much. Whatever we have crafted an idol out of, our tendency is to overindulge in it. Honestly, I felt that gluttony is an issue that is spread across multiple chapters of the book, so to give it an entire chapter on its own seemed redundant.

Envy, another sin on the "original" lists, felt similar (particularly as we talk about greed and entitlement later on). Envy comes out of our discontentment—when we feel like we deserve something that someone else has—and we either feed our desires or allow our hearts to drift to a state of bitterness in which nothing we have is good enough. As we will discuss later, this all comes down to the state of our hearts, not the amount of money in our checking accounts or our relationship status.

Learning How to Live

The origin story for this book comes back to a passage from the apostle Paul's last letter to Timothy, his apprentice and closest partner in ministry, before Paul is to be executed. He is telling Timothy all the final things he wants him to know.

Toward the end of the letter, he gives Timothy some wisdom for how to live.

> But mark this: There will be terrible times in the last days. People will be lovers of themselves, lovers of money, boastful, proud, abusive, disobedient to their parents, ungrateful, unholy, without love, unforgiving, slanderous, without self-control, brutal, not lovers of the good, treacherous, rash, conceited, lovers of pleasure rather than lovers of God—having a form of godliness but denying its power. Have nothing to do with such people. (2 Tim. 3:1–5)

I don't know about you, but as I read that passage Timothy's circumstances do not feel all that different from the fallen world we live in today. But, also like Timothy, we are called to something higher.

CHAPTER 1

PRIDE & HUMILITY

I remember the exact moment when I was called into vocational ministry. I was sitting at my desk in the middle of a Dallas high-rise when I heard God say, "You are going to work for me." I don't know if you would have heard it if you were sitting beside me, but I know I did. Now, here is something you should know about me: if you ask the people who know me best, they will tell you that I am not a big "I heard God say" guy. This time, however, was different. Even today, all these years later, I can only describe the experience as startling.

I called my friend Bo and asked if he could meet me at my house right away. Keep in mind this was during the middle of the workday.

"I'm at work," he responded.

"Is there any way you can leave? Something big just happened, and I need to process it with you." Being the good friend that he was (and is), Bo said he would find a way to make it happen.

We met at my house at 1:30 in the afternoon. As I paced nervously around the living room, I told him, "You are going to want to sit down for this." He was confused (and probably equally nervous), not sure what I was about to tell him. "I think God just called me into ministry," I said.

Bo wasn't surprised at all. He responded with some encouraging words, letting me know that he had seen God move in my life and could affirm God was doing a new work in me.

Just a few years prior to this moment, I was a regular in the Dallas club scene. I was everything wrong with Dallas wrapped in one person. I was pretentious. I was materialistic. I loved to party. I routinely sought affirmation in shallow relationships and one-night stands. Jesus had saved me and changed my heart, and now it seemed he wanted to change my profession. I hastily decided to hire an attorney so I could start a nonprofit. I thought I would raise money and give it away for Jesus. Bo stopped me and wisely encouraged me to pray before doing anything. "If God is calling you to something, he will show you what in his timing," he said.

So I prayed. I prayed every day. I prayed multiple times a day. "God, put me where you want me and help me find contentment there." On the fifth day of praying that prayer, I was walking through the office foyer in Dallas when my phone rang. It was Rick, a pastor from my church. Rick said, "I have a job I want you to consider." I thought he was talking about volunteering somewhere within the church.

"Sure," I said. "Tell me where to be and when."

Rick replied, "No, I mean a *job*. Here at the church."

I sat quietly on the other end of the phone. Then it hit me. "Oh! I get it. You talked to Bo."

Rick, now confused himself, responded, "Who is Bo?"

I said, "Did you know that five days ago I told my friend Bo I thought God was calling me to ministry?" Rick had no idea. As it turns out, Rick was simply praying over a job description, and he said God had brought me to mind.

At the time, almost twenty years ago, my wife and I were dinks (dual income, no kids). She was an elementary PE teacher, and I was in business development for a Fortune 15 company. We were bringing in hundreds of thousands of dollars annually and (sadly) managing to spend it all on whatever we wanted to have and experience. Also, she planned to stay at home when we started our family. This "calling into ministry" was really inconvenient for our plans. We would be transitioning to a single income—a pastor's salary of $40,000. We had a mortgage and would soon have our first child on the way. But you know what? I had no question there was a God. I didn't wonder if I believed in him. He was more real than he had ever been. If he were asking me to do something, why would I not do that?

He called me to something, and he made a way.

I went to work at that church as a small group pastor. Two years in, I started preaching. Over the next few years, a 150-person ministry grew into thousands of participants, with tens of thousands streaming online. Speaking engagement requests came in by the dozens. A publisher called and wanted me to write a book. I had an agent! Who knew pastors had agents?! I was being asked to speak on some of the largest stages in the world and was making close to as much money as I had in the corporate world, which I didn't even know was possible.

One Friday morning I was meeting with the other men in my small group. It was common for us to confess sin to each other and offer prayer for one another. I told them, "I feel as though I'm becoming spiritually arrogant." When I didn't make much money and was the guy setting out chairs, God was so real and my motive was so pure. Now I wasn't so sure. I loved being loved. I loved having fans and followers. Sin had crept in and was starting to wreak havoc throughout my life. I told those guys, "I think I need to wrestle God like Jacob in Genesis 32. He needs to knock my hip out of the socket." So they prayed he would. You will read more about that later, but spoiler: he did.

Too Many Chairs

Have you ever had to put up chairs? I have moved a lot of chairs in the last twenty years. It is an unexpected part of ministry no one warns you about. When God called me to it, I wish he had said, *JP, I want you to quit your job and go work in ministry. PS: make sure you work on your biceps and triceps.* Just a little heads-up would have been nice.

Metal folding chairs, conference center chairs, hotel ballroom chairs . . . I've moved all of them over the years. Whenever it's time to clean up after an event, the same situation unfolds. Different people carry different amounts of chairs. You always have the one guy who is there solely for the social aspect. He carries one at a time and is more focused on finishing his story than he is on getting the chairs on the rack. On the opposite end of the spectrum is the Gym Guy. You all know Gym Guy. He is there to show everyone that he has never missed arm day. He may even do Cross-Fit. You will have to ask him. Gym Guy is going to try to set a Guinness World Record in that moment. Everyone else is just doing their best and trying to carry as many as they can.

Without fail, something happens every single time: somebody drops some chairs. It makes a terrible noise. There is nothing worse than the sound of five metal folding chairs crashing onto a concrete floor. Why did they drop them? They were trying to carry too many. Eventually they lost their grip, one chair started to slide out of their hand, and then the whole stack tumbled to the ground. They thought they had the situation under control, but eventually the whole thing came crashing down on them. They were carrying more than they were meant to carry.

The Vice of Pride

Pride causes us to carry more than we are supposed to, and a crash is coming. Christians believe that pride is at the root of Satan's sin. According to Satan's origin story in Ezekiel 28:12–19, he was an angel—the most decorated and beautiful in God's kingdom. But that wasn't enough for him. He tried to grasp the same authority and power God had, so he was cast out of heaven and sent to earth. At the end of the day, Satan decided that merely being in a relationship with God was not enough. He wanted to *be* God. He did not trust God, and then he made it his mission to cause others to do the same. In *Mere Christianity*, C. S. Lewis wrote,

> According to Christian teachers, the essential vice, the utmost evil, is Pride. Unchastity, anger, greed, drunkenness, and all that, are mere fleabites in comparison: it was through Pride that the devil became the devil: Pride leads to every other vice: it is the complete anti-God state of mind.[1]

The same desire that caused Satan to be cast out of heaven shows up in the garden of Eden in Genesis 3. What Satan offers Eve is not a briefcase full of money or unlimited pleasure; it is the opportunity to be just like God. Satan, from the very beginning of humanity, has used pride to tempt people to want to be like God. It is a consistent story arc throughout the Old Testament: God instructs his people to do something, they decide they know better, they do whatever they want, and then they have to deal with the repercussions of their sin. They loved the idea of playing God. And we do too.

This same theme plays out in the New Testament. In 1 Peter 5:5, Peter writes,

> In the same way, you who are younger, submit yourselves to your elders. All of you, clothe yourselves with humility toward one another, because,
>
> > "God opposes the proud,
> > but shows favor to the humble."

Here, Peter is quoting Proverbs 3:34 to drive a message home to his audience: God doesn't just turn a blind eye to the prideful. He *opposes* them. A few years ago, I wrote this verse on my bathroom mirror and read it every morning to remind me of what is true (more on that later). The clothing metaphor Peter uses here is really easy for us to understand too: we are either wearing pride or we are wearing humility.

When we wear pride, we open ourselves up to sin. Our temptation is to read that sentence, nod our heads, and keep going about our days. But stop and think about that: when we wear pride, we open ourselves to sin. Wearing pride leads to us being *devoured* by sin. Do you remember when Lady

Gaga wore a dress made out of meat to the 2010 MTV Video Music Awards? If you are unfamiliar, it was not a dress that *looked like* meat. She was basically wearing a rib eye. Now imagine placing Lady Gaga in her meat dress in a cage with a lion. How is that going to go? That is what happens when we wear pride.

We have an enemy, Satan, who is not of this world and wants nothing more than for our sin to devour us and destroy our lives. Proverbs 16:18 says, "Pride goes before destruction, a haughty spirit before a fall." Pride is always the predecessor to destruction.

Satan is like a hungry lion. That's interesting to me, because then we have options. So what can we do? We can refuse to feed him. Think of Satan like a stray cat (or stray lion, for the sake of this illustration). What happens when you feed a stray cat? It finds a home. You become a cat owner!

But if you starve him and say, "No, no, no. There's nothing to eat here. I'm not doing that. I'm not looking at that. I'm not going there. I'm not thinking about that," everything shifts. Satan says, "All right. I guess I'll find someone else to feed me. I've got to eat." When he doesn't eat he becomes weak, and when he's weak you can resist him. So don't feed him. You have a choice to feed him or not.

How do you know if you are wearing pride? The easiest way is a self-diagnostic test. Ask yourself a lot of questions. Are you anxious? Are you critical of others? Are you defensive when someone points out the sin in your life? Are you quick to notice pride in others? Do you constantly seek out the approval of others? Are you critical of others? Are you insecure? Do you take advantage of God's grace? Do you feel ashamed? Do you think your sin is bigger than God's grace can handle? Do you believe you are worthless or unforgivable? Does a particular sin define you more than God's claim on your life?

If your answer to any of those questions is yes, then welcome to the club. It is one thing to understand that we struggle with this sin, but it is another to seek healing and restoration from it. I believe this struggle, more than any other sin, can rob you of God's favor, his blessing, his joy, and his grace. I have learned this from experience.

The Lesson I Keep Learning

I distinctly remember the day my parents moved me into my college apartment. We hauled my furniture in. We bought a few groceries. We put out a couple of family pictures. I hugged them goodbye, and as I watched them drive out of the parking lot, the realization hit me: I was free to do *whatever* I wanted. There was a world of endless possibilities at my fingertips. Whatever I wanted to indulge in I could, because I was *free*.

The problem was I had all of the freedom I could ever hope for but no maturity. The very next night I went to a frat party and learned what a "keg stand" was. I chased the party scene. I drank. I did drugs. I hooked up with girls. I began feeding an addiction to pornography. I got a job, which paid me money that I could turn around and use on all of my newfound hobbies. I found myself in a relationship with a girl I thought I loved (based on a very unhealthy definition of the word). As I added all of these new things to my life, I started to push out the church and God at the same time.

One evening, I realized I was carrying too much. I felt different. Far from God. Overcommitted. I needed the approval of others. I was constantly performing and trying to keep up my newfound persona. When I said my prayers (I had years of Catholic school under my belt, so nightly prayers stayed part of my routine), I felt like God wasn't listening.

I laid in my twin-size bed, staring through the dark at the ceiling, and began to weep uncontrollably. What had happened to me?

Fast-forward almost two decades from being dropped off in that dorm room. Just about everything in my life was changed. I had surrendered my life to Christ. Gone was the pornography addiction. The hookups had long been a thing of the past; I was now married with three kids. I was serving on a church staff leading a large young adult ministry. I had started getting speaking requests outside of our church. I had just signed a book deal! Everything was up and to the right. Or so it seemed. Little did I know I was wearing pride. In such moments, pride is like a weighted vest you might wear when working out. It might make you look bigger and stronger, but in truth it is just weighing you down. It's making everything more difficult than it needs to be.

Pride leads to anxiety, because we start thinking *everything* depends on us. We think we are either Superman or Wonder Woman, and if we do not live up to our end of the bargain (you know, saving the world) then we are going to let ourselves, God, and the whole world down. But God never intended it to be that way. The next two verses in 1 Peter 5 say this: "Humble yourselves, therefore, under God's mighty hand, that he may lift you up in due time. Cast all your anxiety on him because he cares for you" (vv. 6–7). You think you have to do it all right now. You need to graduate with a 4.0. You need to be married. You need the corner office, the perfect house in the best neighborhood, the best schools. And wherever you look are people who seem to have it all while you do not, and you just feel further and further behind. But what if you humbled yourself under the mighty hand of God so that in his timing he might lift you up?

In *his* timing he might lift you up. Sometimes, when it feels like the hand of God is holding you back or crushing you, he is actually protecting you so that when he's ready he can say, "OK, experience this."

During the summer of 2017, I thought I had to do it all myself. I thought I was invincible. I had heard about people getting burned out, but I thought I was immune. I would think, *That's too bad for them. I don't even know what they're talking about. I can't even relate to that.* Sounds humble, right? Then I had a family member get sick and began to care for them and help them. That happened in the midst of a busy summer teaching schedule during which I taught twenty-five times in six weeks. In the middle of that came my book deal, so then I had deadlines to meet and obligations to fulfill.

In the midst of *that*, I went down to a church in Austin and taught three messages back to back to back. As I was driving back to Dallas, a large church on the West Coast called and said, "Hey, we'd love for you to come teach here next Sunday." I couldn't believe it. What an honor! I said, "This is amazing. I'd love to do that." All the while, I began to feel pride swell up in me. These were all great opportunities too. Kingdom-advancing opportunities—but good things become bad things if we try to carry too many things.

I really felt like Superman during that season. As I mentioned earlier, I even told my small group about feeling some pride in myself and reading the story of Jacob in Genesis 32. God knocked Jacob's hip out of socket, and from that moment forward he walked with a limp. I asked my small group to pray that God would humble me. Public service announcement: be careful with that prayer. He just might do it.

I flew out to teach at that church in California. The night before I was supposed to teach, when I was lying in my too-small hotel room bed, my heart started pounding. *Bum bum ba-doom! Bum bum ba-doom!* I thought, *Something is wrong with my heart. What's wrong with me? Something is not right with my heart. What's wrong with my heart?* Then I started going down that path, thinking, *I have to sleep. I have to get up in front of a bunch of people tomorrow. I have to sleep. I need sleep. Something is wrong with my heart. I need to sleep. What's going on?* Have you ever been in that cycle? All you can think about is how you need sleep, so it makes you anxious when you cannot sleep, and it becomes a never-ending cycle.

I finally got through that terrible night and pushed through giving my message the next morning. They were in a series there called "Everyday Heroes," and they had a picture of Superman. A guy got up after me and thanked me by saying, "Was that not amazing? That guy reminds me of Superman." I heard that from backstage and I thought, *Superman? I can't even fall asleep like a normal person. I'm definitely not leaping over buildings. What's wrong with me?*

When I flew back to Dallas, something still was not right. Finally, I could not take it anymore, and I went to the emergency room. When I got there, I told the medical staff,

"Something is wrong with my heart." All the while, these waves of overwhelming anxiety just came crashing over me. I could *feel* them. This was different from worrying; this was heavier than that. My anxiety was overwhelming. They hooked me up for EKGs and a bunch of other tests, and then the doctor said, "Yeah, your heart is not beating right. There are some PVCs (premature ventricular contractions)."

I looked at the doctor and said, "You've got to fix it." Then the doctor asked, "Are you carrying too much? Are you stressed?"

At the time I didn't know I was, but let me go ahead and put on some humility: that moment, sitting in a hospital room hooked up to machines, was the answer to prayer. Pride for me looked like a savior complex. Sure, my intentions started off pure. I felt like I needed to save everyone. I needed to say yes to every situation. I needed to control every facet of my life. It looked like taking on more than I could handle but not realizing it. Even my loved ones said things like, "You're doing too much. I don't know that you need to be everywhere." But I felt like I did.

Pride looked like finding my identity in silly, worldly things like book deals and big churches, and the Lord humbled me. He said, *You're going to wear* this, *JP.* My heart still skips beats at times. It serves as a reminder not to take on too much. Do you know why he did it? Because he loves me. I say it's better to wear the hand of God than anxiety.

The Virtue of Humility

You've likely heard it said that humility is not just thinking less of yourself but thinking of yourself less. That is true, and it is a great first step in learning to wear humility. But humility is also more than that. Biblical humility is not just thinking of yourself less but also thinking of others more or thinking more of others.

My ditch (the thing that is going to get me in trouble if I am left to my own devices) is that I tend to think I can do anything better than someone else, even someone whom God created to do those things. That is not a fun thing to share, especially in the pages of a book. But it is true. How that plays out in my life and leadership is *control*. I want to speak into everything. I want my hands in everything. In my pride, my flesh, I think I can do things better. And that's not right. It's not godly, and it is the opposite of humility.

Every year I read a book (but just one). Just kidding—I read that same book year in and year out. It's called *The Freedom of Self-Forgetfulness* by Timothy Keller. It's a really short book that I have found to be helpful over and over again in my life. One of the things it talks about is the problem of pride. You can identify it this way: Do you need to make every conversation about yourself? When you are interacting with someone and they say, "Yeah, well, my kid just got their report card . . ." and you say, "Oh, well, let me tell you about *my* kid and *their* report card," or they say, "Yeah, we're thinking about moving . . ." and you immediately interject with, "Oh, we moved once. We got a house, also," you are pivoting each conversation back to yourself, and something is off.

I say that so passionately because I've experienced this firsthand. I noticed at one point, after being in ministry for a while, that so much of my time was just helping people. They would line up and say, "Well, here's my marriage. Here's my kid. Here's my situation. Here are my struggles. Here's my addiction. Can you help me? Can you help me? Can you help me?" I found so much identity in helping others solve their problems, and I didn't even realize it.

I moved myself into a socially awkward place; I would go to a Super Bowl or Christmas party, and if someone wasn't asking me for help, I didn't know what to talk about. They would say, "Hey, man, did you see that game? How about this?" I'd say, "No. How's your marriage?" I know; I was a blast at parties. It's like everything needed to be a pastoral care situation. Realizing that not everyone needed my help all of the time was humiliating—it brought about humility in my life.

Humility seems like a benign virtue. It is highly likely that when you woke up this morning, your first prayer was not, "Lord, please make me more humble. I just want more humility in my life." However, I had a profound revelation when studying humility: it is vital to our spiritual, emotional, and mental health. I believe that the secret to happiness is actually practicing humility. Without humility, we can be driven to a place where we think about ourselves all the time. Mental illness is often (not always, but often) born out of pride. We can move to a place of misery. But with humility, we're able to lose our lives and hold this world loosely. Only with humility can we really live the Christian life as it was intended.

We're able to serve others joyfully, to get outside of our own heads and assess the needs of others and how we can best care for one another. It really shifts everything to believe that happiness is more tied to humility than anything. When we preface things we say with, "Hey, this might sound prideful, but . . ." we don't realize that what's about to come out of our mouths is destructive. We must learn to take those thoughts captive, imprison them, and execute them, lest they carry us somewhere wicked and evil. If we define greatness as anything other than humble service to the humblest man to ever live, we've made the same mistake as the devil.

The Example of Jesus

Christians look to Jesus as the example to follow in everything we say and do. As Hebrews 12:2 says, Jesus is both the pioneer (or maybe your version says "founder" or "author") and perfecter of our faith. So, as we try to grow in the virtue of humility, our search starts and ends with Jesus. The entire narrative of Jesus's life is one of humility from the very beginning. Think about it: the very notion that God would become human by being born of a humble virgin in a humble stable in a humble, sleepy little town like Bethlehem is enough right there. But that is just the beginning of Jesus exemplifying humility during his time on earth.

Once his earthly ministry began, Jesus consistently found ways to out-serve and out-honor those around him. Even as his disciples started to quibble about who among them was the greatest (an odd thing to argue about when you live beside the Messiah), Jesus responded with his own personal mission statement in Mark 10:45, saying, "The Son of Man did not come to be served, but to serve, and to give his life as a ransom for many."

Humility, for Jesus, came through service to those around him. The night of the Last Supper, right before Jesus was to be tortured and crucified, he took time to wash the disciples' feet (John 13:1–17). This humble act, even to the disciples, felt so . . . wrong. Peter even objected to it! But Jesus was making a point. In the upside-down world of the gospel, leadership is service. It is dying to yourself and your preferences. It is swallowing your pride. It is getting your hands dirty to serve those around you. It is a different way of living.

Jesus's humility did not end there. As he, a sinless man, was beaten, tortured, and mocked all the way to the cross, he did it all with humility. The apostle Paul, in his letter to the Philippians, described Jesus like this:

> And being found in appearance as a man,
> he humbled himself
> by becoming obedient to death—
> even death on a cross! (2:8)

Jesus made himself *nothing*. Even on the cross—the worst, most gruesome way the Roman Empire would execute someone. Your hands and feet would be pierced. You would have to push up on the nail driven through your feet so you could breathe. You would die this slow, humiliating death by asphyxiation. It was only for the most heinous of criminals who committed the most heinous crimes.

Jesus, who was fully God, pushed aside his unlimited power. The most powerful King did not use what was available to him to free himself but rather used it to serve others. This King died for his kingdom—but the kingdom he died for killed him.

Dressing for the Day

Remember the call from 1 Peter 5:5 to clothe yourself with humility? Here is the thing about humility: it looks good on everyone. Humility is always appropriate. You can wear it with a tux or your favorite little black dress. You can wear it with jeans and boots or shorts and flip-flops. Whatever situation you walk into, wearing humility will always de-escalate it from the start. It is what Jesus would do.

I remember a couple of years ago I had a meeting on my calendar with someone I found myself rather frustrated with. I don't know if you've ever done this, but I rehearsed the entire conversation in my head. I was perfecting all of my comebacks to each of his arguments, and I found myself getting worked up. Right before the meeting, I walked into my closet to get dressed. In such moments I always try to think, *What will help me further the gospel? What won't be a hindrance? What should I wear?*

In that moment I felt the conviction of the Holy Spirit: *Clothe yourself in humility. You're going to have to put on a lot of humility for this one. You need to put aside your agenda. You need to go with a heart to listen. You need to seek to understand.*

In every conflict I've been a part of, when I am able to do that, things turn out to not be as I first saw them. The motive was not as it seemed. And sure enough, after that meeting, he and I were able to pursue unity, march forward in oneness, and advance the kingdom together. I'm confident that, had the Holy Spirit not been so kind as to remind me of that verse, I would have hindered that outcome.

When Jesus's disciples argued among themselves about who was the greatest among them, Jesus's answer wasn't what they hoped for. He did not wink at one of them or stop the entire conversation to rank them in order. He had already told them in Luke 7:28 that "among those born of women there is no one greater than John [the Baptist]." You know, the guy who wore clothes made out of camel hair and ate locusts. That guy was the greatest. Why? John used his entire life to point people to the greatness of Jesus. He leveraged everything he had so that people would know about Jesus.

I do not think, when we get to heaven, we are going to be able to say, "God, why didn't you tell me? I wouldn't have gotten so lost in my business. I wouldn't have cared so much about my money. I wouldn't have been so consumed with my grades. I wouldn't have gotten so lost in relationships. I wouldn't have been so wrapped up in getting Instagram followers had you just told me. Why didn't you just tell me? If you wanted me to be like John the Baptist, why didn't you just say that he was the greatest human ever born?" He'll say, "Why didn't you just read the Bible?"

I think there is still hope for each of us. This could be a turning point, right now. You could close this book and say, "In every relationship, from this moment on until I'm face-to-face with Jesus, I'm going to seek to lose myself in order to serve others and care for those around me." If you have ever met someone who does that, I'm sure you really enjoy them. So there are benefits for you too—but don't do it for the benefits; do it to *be like Jesus.*

THREE QUESTIONS TO ASK YOURSELF

1. How do you struggle with pride in your life?

2. Do you think of the people around you often, or do you find yourself more consumed by your own thoughts, feelings, wants, and desires?

3. How can you take a step in growing in humility today?

CHAPTER 2

ANGER & FORGIVENESS

In my own BC (before Christ) days, I had an anger problem. If you met me today, that would surprise you, but those were different times. I would suppress my emotions. I'd kind of bottle up the jealousy, or whatever was going on in my heart, and then at some point explode in a violent act or loud outburst, especially when things didn't go my way. Sporting events or any kind of competition could break out into a fight. Both friendships and dating relationships would end in angry explosions. Whenever I heard stories of relationships ending amicably or someone said something about a "mutual breakup," I just assumed they were lying. That was a completely foreign concept to me.

One of those BC fights stands out in particular to me even today. I grew up in a small town (Cuero, Texas). Think six thousand people in the middle of nowhere. I worked in a neighboring city (Victoria), which was a little larger but not a metropolitan area by any stretch of the imagination. I lived in Cuero but worked in Victoria, at a car wash (making bank, obviously). I traveled back and forth a lot, and I had one friend in Victoria who said I could stay with him on the weekends, which meant I didn't have to drive back and forth all the time. He gave me a place to live. That's a good friend.

One weekend, all of my friends were going to go to the big water park about an hour and a half away. When I say "big water park," some of you think I'm talking about a couple of water slides or something. Get that out of your head. This place was perfect—a teenager's dream. A beautiful, wonderful place. Uphill water coasters, lazy rivers, wave pools, you name it. And all of my friends were going, so I told the guy I was living with, "Hey, we should go too." He said, "I can't. I don't have any money." My generous spirit kicked in.

I said, "Oh, buddy. You don't understand. I'm gettin' paid over there at the car wash. I've got you, bro. I'm going. You're going. We're going! I'll pay your way in. That's what friends do." So off we go to the water park of our dreams and have a fantastic time being lazy in the river and going down tube slides and getting a little glimpse of what heaven may be like. Then, as we were leaving, my friend went into the gift shop and came out with a brand-new puka shell necklace. You know the necklace . . . the kind with tiny white shells. Some of you had one. Some of you are wearing one right now. This one was even better—it also had a little shark tooth dangling down in the middle.

I could not believe it. After I paid his way in with my car wash money! I said, "Whoa, whoa, whoa. What's that? What are you doing wearing that necklace? Why did you get that?" He said, "Oh, man, I saw it and I had to have it. Isn't it amazing? It's puka shells." I said, "But you didn't have money for a ticket in here." He replied, "Yeah, I didn't have the money for the ticket in here, but I *really* wanted this necklace."

I had done a little reconnaissance work that day. I had *also* noticed the puka shell necklace with the shark tooth hanging in the middle (who wouldn't?). I knew it cost approximately the same price I'd paid for his ticket. I said, "Listen here. If I'm paying your ticket in, you can't go spending money on a necklace."

There we were in the parking lot of the most magical place in Texas, going back and forth. Then I gave him a little shove. In my seventeen-year-old mind, I thought he would give me a little shove back, maybe we would exchange some light blows, and then we'd get up, put our arms around each other, and say, "All right. Let's go home." You know, we were tired. We'd been in the hot Texas sun all day, so we wouldn't fight for too long.

What happened, in reality, is he got up from my shove and said, "We're done. Don't call me. Get your stuff out of my house. I never want to see you again." I was taken aback. But I knew hurt people hurt people, so I thought he was just talking crazy. I called him the next day, ready to make it right. No answer. I kept calling, and finally his mom answered. I said, "Hey, it's me. May I speak to your son, please?" I really turned on the charm. She said, "Oh, he never wants to talk to you again." *Ouch*.

You Are Angrier Than You Realize

What I have learned as I have gotten older is that more people have issues with anger than they realize. Some of you may have even seen the title of this chapter and thought it was one to skip, but here's why you shouldn't: you probably are not as good at handling your anger as you think you are. It is easy to see it in the boss who explodes over small mistakes or the parent who blows up on a Little League umpire over an iffy strike call. We are pretty good at pointing out the speck in their eye while missing the log in our own (Matt. 7:1–3). For many of us, anger manifests itself differently. We let small frustrations build up around us and within us, and we end up carrying around much more anger than we realize.

Have you ever been stopped at a traffic light, the light turns green, it takes you all of two seconds to go from the brake to the accelerator, but someone behind you honks their horn at you? There is something really offensive about a honk. You might as well be cursing at me to my face! Or maybe your roommates (or your kids) drive you crazy, and you find yourself just locking yourself in your room because that is easier than dealing with them face-to-face. Maybe your anger comes up in your marital relationship. You coexist in this always tense, passive-aggressive world where you take subtle (and not-so-subtle) jabs at each other. Maybe it happens in your parenting. Your two-year-old won't eat their carrots (which can be a tough sell), while your four-year-old won't stay in their seat. Maybe your sixteen-year-old is acting like you did when you were sixteen.

Whatever your default posture toward conflict is, it was (most likely) shaped by the home you grew up in. This chapter will hit everyone differently based on the way those who raised you approached anger, conflict, and forgiveness. Some of you had parents who were extremely passive-aggressive. Some were peace-fakers. Some were peace-breakers. Some of them would just yell and throw things, so you learned to do that too. It was passed on to you like a relay baton. You have to trust me: you will take that relay baton, and you will pass it on to your children. That's the way this works. Some of you have been going through life with your great-great-great-grandfather's anger problem, and you didn't even know it. But there *is* another way.

Jesus says this is a really big deal. In the Sermon on the Mount, the greatest sermon of all time, he basically says, "The way you deal with anger will impact the way you will be judged. Those of you who are angry will incur a stricter judgment. You will be judged for that" (see Matt. 5:22). Whether we are prone to explosions or used to stuffing our anger away, we all need to learn the appropriate way to approach anger and forgiveness because it *really* matters to Jesus. In Paul's second letter to the church at Corinth, he tells them:

> All this is from God, who reconciled us to himself through Christ and gave us the ministry of reconciliation: that God was reconciling the world to himself in Christ, not counting people's sins against them. And he has committed to us the message of reconciliation. We are therefore Christ's ambassadors, as though God were making his appeal through us. We implore you on Christ's behalf: Be reconciled to God. God made him who had no sin to be sin for us, so that in him we might become the righteousness of God. (2 Cor. 5:18–21)

Paul is saying that all believers are placed here to be ambassadors for Christ; we are Jesus's PR firm on earth. But that's not all! We have a "ministry of reconciliation." We put broken pieces back together. As those who have been reconciled to God, we should be leading the charge when it comes to forgiving the sins of others because we have been forgiven of much. We should be the best in the world at restoring relationships because our relationship with Jesus has been restored. This all begins with viewing each conflict we are part of as an opportunity, not an obstacle.

Every Conflict Is an Opportunity

My wife drives a Suburban, and if the check engine light comes on, that light is telling her something is wrong with her vehicle. She can respond to it in one of three ways, two of them being the wrong way. One option is to ignore it. She can sit there and say, "You know, a lot of people's check engine lights are on. I'm sure it's fine." Another option is to overreact to it. "My check engine light came on? We need to sell this thing. Leave this piece of trash here and let's go."

The third option is to do the right thing, which is to figure out what's going on inside all those components that are causing the problem. If she ignores it, it's going to continue to break down and get more expensive, but if she sees it and says, "I'm going to put in the work to find out what's going on," she'll probably be able to diagnose the problem and work toward a solution.

Your anger is like a check engine light. When you feel that emotion, it's telling you, *Something's off. I'm angry. Something's off.* We can ignore it and let it build up. We can overreact to it and lash out. Or we can commit to doing the hard work, responding in the Spirit, and asking, "What is going on inside of me that is making me so angry right now?"

You see, every conflict we are a part of is an opportunity, even though many of us do not think of it as one. Conflict is not something we have to avoid, and it's not inherently bad. It is morally neutral, but it *can be* good depending on how we respond to it. If we avoid it, that's a poor response, and if we blow up, that's also a poor response. But we can choose to view each conflict as an opportunity to be sanctified, to glorify God, to grow as a Christian, and to heal a relationship. We have a lot of great opportunities in the midst of conflict.

Some of the greatest entrepreneurs in the world see problems as opportunities. When the rest of the world throws their arms up, these folks come around the problem and say, "How can we solve this problem and capitalize on this situation?" In that same way, some of the most committed Christians in the world see conflict as an opportunity to be an ambassador of reconciliation, to heal relationships, and to restore those relationships to the point where they are even stronger than they were before the conflict began. That conflict in your marriage is an opportunity for your marriage to be stronger than it was yesterday. That conflict with your sorority sister is an opportunity for you to become closer friends. It is *always* an opportunity.

Leaving Your Gift at the Altar

Jesus doesn't mess around when it comes to resolving conflict quickly. Here is what he says during the Sermon on the Mount:

> Therefore, if you are offering your gift at the altar and there remember that your brother or sister has something against you, leave your gift there in front of the altar. First go and be reconciled to them; then come and offer your gift. (Matt. 5:23–24)

I think we read that, and we're like, "OK, that is not applicable to us, because we've never brought any gift to an altar."

The people listening to Jesus preach this sermon, however, would have brought a sacrifice, a burnt, fragrant offering, to the Lord's altar as a way of saying, "God, forgive us." Jesus is telling them, "Before you seek *my* forgiveness, you go seek *their* forgiveness." In other words, "Before you come to me, asking me to forgive you, you need to go to them and ask them to forgive you."

Jesus places these words in prime real estate, toward the beginning of the most famous sermon of all time. This is basically Jesus saying, "I really want you to know this is important. Our relationship can't be right unless your other relationships are right." This is why we see this repeated in the Scriptures, just in case we were to say, "Well, that's just one rogue spot." Nope. In the Lord's Prayer, Jesus also says, "Forgive us our debts [that's our sins], as we also have forgiven our debtors" (6:12). Our offering and seeking for-giveness to and from others always goes hand in hand with our seeking forgiveness from God.

Here's what this means: you may need to put this book down and go seek reconciliation. If that's you, go! ("Is he talking to me?" YES!) You need to pick up the phone. You may even need to buy a plane ticket. You need to sit in front of someone and say, "Would you forgive me? This relation-ship is not right. I know I wronged you when . . ." It's so evident in the Scriptures that this is what Jesus is asking of us. Could it be any clearer?

Understanding Forgiveness

My friend Ally taught me a lesson in forgiveness a few years ago. We were about to go on a mission trip to Brazil. We were going to be traveling via plane, then by boat for a few days until we got to the tribe we were going to share the gospel with. The airline had a very strict fifty-pound limit for luggage (you know the drill), and we had talked about that no less than ten times leading up to the trip.

As you might expect, when we made it to the airport Ally's bag weighed in at fifty-four pounds. As we did the suitcase shuffle (you've all done it), I stood over to the side while she looked for what could be the thing tipping her bag over the scales. After about ninety seconds, she pulled out (I kid you not) an actual bag of rocks. I was so confused. Were these special rocks? Was she afraid they wouldn't have rocks in Brazil? Really, why the rocks? I could tell she was embarrassed, so I didn't want to draw attention to it at the moment. But I was so curious!

She pulled me aside before the flight took off and told me she was going through a recovery ministry, and each rock represented a person in her life she needed to forgive but had not yet. I was taken aback—what a powerful illustration! That is exactly what bitterness is: baggage we carry around and let weigh us down.

A few days went by, and God was moving on this trip. We were worshiping on the deck of the boat one evening right as the sun was setting, and out of the corner of my eye I saw Ally walk to the edge of the boat, rocks in hand. One by one, she threw each one into the Amazon River, with tears streaming down her face as she let go of each wrong that still had a hold on her heart. Each piece of bitterness and resentment, she threw out into the river. She then came back to the group and asked me to baptize her in that very water.

You see, Ally understood that forgiveness is not optional for followers of Jesus. To rightly understand forgiveness, we always have to start with Jesus. He has accounted for our sin against a holy God. And who our sin is against matters. Follow me here: if you trespass on my lawn, I may call the police after the third or fourth time you do it, but if you trespass on the White House lawn, you are going to be shot.

You see, who the offense is against matters. Our offense was against a holy God. The punishment we deserve is hell. We've been adulterous and murderous in our thoughts. We've been vengeful. And through it all, he has forgiven us. We have to start our forgiveness of someone else by looking at the cross and living out Jesus's example. He didn't ignore our sin. He took an account of it. He said, "This is your sin, and this is what it cost," and he paid for it. In doing so, he wiped our debt clean.

To forgive someone in your life, you are going to take an account of what their sin cost you emotionally. "This is how you have hurt me and what you have done." Then you are going to say, "I forgive you, which means I will not seek revenge for that emotional damage." Now, if they've hurt your car or property, or they have to serve a sentence, forgiveness does not mean those consequences disappear. It doesn't mean they shouldn't pay for it or make arrangements through insurance to take care of it, but as far as the emotional damage they have caused you goes, you are no longer going to hold on to bitterness against them.

Now, here is what that *doesn't* mean. It doesn't mean you aren't going to set boundaries. It doesn't mean you aren't going to be wise in your interactions moving forward. It doesn't mean forgetting what happened. It's crazy that some people think forgiving means forgetting. We can't forget something outside of a brain surgery like a lobotomy. It's humanly impossible. But forgiving is to take an account and say, "This is how you have hurt me and what your hurt cost me, and I'm telling you that you don't have to pay me back. I have erased that debt."

When You Are the Offender

Listen, I understand it is counterintuitive to admit when you're wrong. There is something deep inside each of us that wants to always be in the right, regardless of whether or not we really are. But there are going to be times you hurt those around you. You will say something in your flesh that tears down someone else. You will respond with anger. You will make a sarcastic comment that cuts deeper than you thought it would. All of these things are normal, but that doesn't make them OK. Earlier in Matthew 5, Jesus says, "Blessed are the peacemakers, for they will be called children of God" (v. 9). Those of us who are children of God are called to be peacemakers. Not peace-fakers who pretend like nothing is ever wrong. Not peace-breakers who sow discord wherever they go. We are called to be peacemakers, and an important first step in that is knowing how to ask for forgiveness.

Please understand that in any conflict you're involved in, you have a part to own. Maybe it is 90 percent. Or your percentage might be 2 percent. It might be 50 percent or 33 percent, but in every conflict is a piece you can own, and you often have to work to figure out what that is. I don't care if they kicked your dog or used your toothbrush or used your toothbrush to wash the dog. Or maybe they said something really mean and untrue about you. If you're a part *of* the conflict, you most likely have a part *in* the conflict. It is up to you to own 100 percent of whatever your part in the conflict is.

What I should have done at the water park is gone up to my friend and said, "Man, sweet shark tooth necklace. Bro, I wanted that too. Hey, will you please forgive me? When I gave you the money for that ticket, I didn't realize I attached some strings to it. I really thought you wouldn't spend money on anything else, but I didn't communicate that to you, which means I put expectations on you that I never talked about. Will you please forgive me?"

That phrase right there is so vitally important: "Will you please forgive me?" It starts with a *will*, which implies a question. When you simply say, "I'm sorry," it carries no weight. It sounds like the halfhearted apologies you gave to your siblings growing up when your mom forced you to apologize, and it can be empty words. "I'm sorry" just doesn't get the job done. The other person could be like, "You're right. You are sorry! What you did was sorry!"

Another thing: "Forgive me for_____" is a command. You're still trying to be in charge. For there to be a true request for forgiveness on your part, you have to be willing to relinquish control. "Forgive me. Forgive me for whatever I did. Forgive *me* for *you* being so sensitive. Forgive me that you interpreted what I did the wrong way." Don't do that.

I would also encourage you to avoid the "Forgive me if_____." The *if* lacks ownership. It makes it seem like you haven't taken the time to determine if you've actually caused hurt or not.

Here's what you do (and it requires a completely different posture). "Will you please forgive me for_____?" Those are really powerful words that will change your life if you take them with you. "Will you please forgive me for_____?" The next time you have the opportunity (and remember, every conflict is an opportunity) to say that to someone, it's going to be really, really difficult, because the spiritual war is real and Satan hates you. He is going to try to give you every reason you can imagine to leave the conflict unresolved or to convince you to double down on your own correctness.

Every one of us is going to be in a situation where we have the opportunity to say, "Will you please forgive me for_____?" and it's going to be so hard. But it will also be so good.

When You Are the Offended One

People will inevitably hurt you. It may be a spouse, a co-worker, a sibling, or a pastor, but someone is going to say or do something that wounds you, whether or not that was their intent. The temptation will be to hold on to those hurts, not resolve them, and walk around carrying unspoken bitterness and anger. But what if there was a way to quickly resolve it? The fastest way to move toward forgiveness is to go to the person who wronged you. I know that may sound scary, but it is the *biblical* way to begin the process. After all, in another example of Jesus talking about resolving conflict, he says,

> If your brother or sister sins, go and point out their fault, just between the two of you. If they listen to you, you have won them over. But if they will not listen, take one or two others along, so that "every matter may be established by

the testimony of two or three witnesses." If they still refuse to listen, tell it to the church; and if they refuse to listen even to the church, treat them as you would a pagan or a tax collector. (Matt. 18:15–17)

I have another phrase that is going to change your life—at least as it relates to resolving conflict. After you have sought their forgiveness for your part (and remember, you always have a part to own), your next phrase is, "You hurt me by_____." Then you articulate how they wounded you. It really is that simple.

But what if it is hard to explain the hurt you feel? Here are some questions that might help you know what to say. Ask yourself these questions in your quiet time, and ask the Holy Spirit to help you put your feelings into words:

- How do I feel?
- How did they make me feel?
- Am I discouraged?
- Am I hurt?
- Am I angry?
- Am I jealous?
- What did their hurt toward me cost me, and what am I asking for from them?
- What do I think would make this right? (Hopefully it's forgiveness, but if it's not, you can be honest with yourself and begin to process that.)

Once you have thought through these questions and attached answers to them, you will go into your conversation better equipped to extend forgiveness to the other person involved.

Years ago I heard about a young man who'd grown up in an abusive home. Before going any further in the story, let me be clear: abuse of any kind is never OK. Never. His father was an alcoholic and a very angry man, and he took that anger out on his mom. As a little boy, this young man would hide behind the stove and hear that violence, and that was his whole childhood. Then, when he was about eight years old, his dad found his hiding spot. From that point forward, his drunk father took his anger out on him. That was his life. These unjust beatings (obviously) impacted him, and he grew up to be a very angry and bitter human being.

He was speaking to this Christian therapist one day, and the therapist said, "Your anger is impacting your health a great deal. It's hurting you. We need to figure out a path forward. You're going to need to find a way to forgive your dad." The young man just exploded in anger and rage. "How dare you? Did you not hear? Do you not understand what he did? What does that even look like?" But once he calmed down, he asked, "What could I do?"

This Christian therapist said, "Is there any part you can own?"

He exploded again. "You shouldn't even be licensed! I'm never coming to see you again! How dare you? Did you not hear me? He beat me! What is wrong with you? He beat me!" But even as he said those things, his heart softened. He calmed down and said, "What do you mean, own my part?"

The therapist said, "The abuse is not your fault, but as you think back through the years, is there anything you can own?

Have you done anything hateful to your dad? Have you said anything terrible about him? Have you thought murderous thoughts against him? If the entire conflict is 100 percent, I understand that he is the one at fault, but is there any percentage you can own?"

He thought it over and said, "I mean, maybe 2 percent."

"OK," the therapist said. "Just go own 100 percent of your 2 percent, and that will lay the groundwork for you to then express your hurt to him."

The Holy Spirit continued to move in this young man's heart, and he finally worked up the courage to face his dad about the terrible, heinous things his dad had done. He went to him and said, "Dad, I've hated you every day of my life. I've said the most terrible things about you. I've wished you were dead. I've fantasized about hurting you countless times. I'm sorry. Will you please forgive me for thinking these things and feeling these things toward you for all this time? Dad, I need to let you know you hurt me . . ."

Before he could get the last sentence out, the Spirit of God moved, and his dad fell to his knees and then was face-down on the ground, and he just began to weep, saying, "I'm so sorry. I'm so sorry. I'm so sorry." Once his dad finally recovered, he listed everything he had done throughout the years. The son was able to offer him forgiveness. This impossible situation became a son reconciled to his father through the very difficult task of a son expressing his hurt to the person who hurt him. As a friend of mine says, some things are clear in instruction yet complicated in implementation.

Now, here is the important disclaimer: if you are the victim of abuse, I do not in any way want to communicate that you are responsible for what happened to you. No one deserves abuse. No one. What happened to you was wrong, and maintaining healthy boundaries is important. Candidly, as this story was told to me, I was surprised by the therapist's counsel. The son was a victim and was not in any way responsible for his abuse. That's important to make clear.

My takeaway from hearing that story is when hurts go unchecked, they can turn into deep-seated anger. One person's sin can easily cause another person to sin if it is not dealt with. I am not saying anger from abuse is sin. It can, however, cause us to sin.

Jesus has given us a process to deal with anger that keeps those hurts from festering. He loves to see his people reconciled. When we've trusted in Jesus and his payment for our sins, we can be reconciled to God and live as ministers of reconciliation, helping God put the pieces back together again. It's like he's given us a superpower. We can heal relationships. That's huge! I know it is much easier said than done. I know there are many nuances to the hurt you've experienced. As I write this, I am praying for your healing, and I do not want to be flippant about it. I want you to know there's hope and healing ahead. I'd encourage you to process your hurts with other Christians who know and understand the Bible. This is what Jesus has called us to do, and I pray we will find the abundant life and healing he desires when we do so.

THREE QUESTIONS TO ASK YOURSELF

1. How do you struggle with anger in your life?

2. Having read this chapter, do you think you might be angrier than you previously thought? Are you carrying around emotional baggage and bitterness that you honestly hadn't realized was there?

3. How can you take a step in growing in forgiveness today?

CHAPTER 3

GREED & GENEROSITY

These days, a lot of people have a hard time finding a job right after they graduate from college. I'm not here to brag, but when I graduated I had two jobs. Really, no big deal—don't treat me differently. I was living in Waco, Texas, waiting tables at an Italian restaurant and also selling shoes at a store in the mall. Before you get too jealous of my career(s), there is more. I was living with my best friend's parents because my lease had just expired at my duplex. At this point, the highest amount I had ever put on a W-2 was about $7,900—that was the year they gave commission on the shoe sales. I only thought I was making bank at the car wash. Now I was really getting paid. But I wanted more.

One day I woke up earlier than normal, put on some khakis and a polo (even tucked it in), and thought, *I am going to find a* real *job today.* I left the house early that morning and soon was driving around Waco and trying to think it through. *OK. What is it? Where do I go? What do I want to*

*do? Do I just go knock on a door and say, "Hey, will you
please employ me?" Should I look for "Help Wanted" signs
in the window? Should I just show up and start working
and act like I have already been hired?* I had a lot of options.

Keep in mind, I was a college graduate at this point; I had
just finished a two-year art degree from the local technical
college, so you would think my services would be in high
demand. The career office at the college had even said, "If
you go here and you graduate, then we will find a job for
you." Now was the time for them to hold up their end of the
deal! The problem was, I had been so terrible at all things
academically that they couldn't. They basically said, "You
are hopeless. Good luck."

That is how I ended up driving around Waco with no
clue where to go, so I ended up at the mall where I already
had a job. That was the only place I knew to go! I walked
up to the front door to try to find a new, better job, but the
door was locked because the mall wasn't even open yet. Side
note—have you ever been the first one to the mall? That is
a low feeling.

There I was, sitting in the parking lot, and I started praying (which is interesting because this was before I was walking with Jesus, but that was all I knew to do). I said, "Lord,
would you please help me find a job? God, would you please,
please give me a job? Please help me find a job. Any job."
And when the mall eventually opened, I went in and started
walking down the hallway, and this woman came up to me
completely out of the blue and said, "Hey, what is your
story?" Clearly, she was impressed that I had tucked in my
polo that day. I said, "My story is I am looking for a job."
Why not just be honest, right?

She said, "Do you want to manage an Abercrombie & Fitch?" And I said, "Absolutely I do!" And she said, "Where?" I said, "How about Dallas?" And she said, "OK, great. I will get you an interview." I thought, *Is this how prayer works? This is amazing! I should do this more often.* It was hard not to get excited about the thought of being a manager. That was always the person I reported to. Now I could be one of them!

I went to Dallas for my big interview at North Park Mall. If you are unfamiliar with Dallas, North Park is *the* mall you want to be at. I met with this guy there, then got in my car feeling like it had gone well, but it was out of my hands at that point. As I drove the ninety minutes back to Waco, it seemed like the rest of my life hinged on this decision. I was asking all of my friends to pray that this would work out (because I had just learned that prayer works, obviously). I was back at my best friend's parents' house when I got the phone call.

They said, "Mr. Pokluda? We would like to invite you to join our team as an assistant manager at the North Park Abercrombie & Fitch." I was beside myself. It's difficult to put into words the joy I felt in that moment. I said, "Oh, my goodness. This is the greatest news ever. I accept!" Then it got better (if you can even imagine that). The guy on the other end of the line said, "And we are prepared to offer you a salary of $23,000 a year."

When I got off the phone, my best friend ran in the room, and I looked at him and said, "Dude, I've made it. I've made it!" And we did this awkward high-five hug thing that I haven't done with anyone since. We embraced for way too long. I started crying. I was sniffling into his neck. When we separated, he asked the most important question: "How much are they paying?" I said, "You're not going to believe it—23 Gs." I was right, he couldn't believe it. He said, "What are you going to do with all that money?" I didn't even have an answer for him. Who could ever spend that much money?

Fast-forward a little bit, and I'd packed up all of my things and made the move to Dallas. At this point, I was thinking somebody was probably going to make a movie about this small-town boy who moved to the big city to be the assistant manager at Abercrombie. I started working there—and it was terrible. I quit three months later. Next I got a commission-based job at 24 Hour Fitness selling gym memberships. I started making even more money than I had made at Abercrombie. It was exponentially better than my previous job. That really began a long journey of me just looking for the next best thing. Whatever I had, I wanted more. It was like a game to me at this point.

One day this well-dressed guy walked into the gym. He threw his BMW keys on my desk and paid in full for the most expensive membership we offered. Buying this one made you a member for the rest of your life. You could go to any club, any time you want. I was intrigued by this guy, so I said, "What do you do for a living?" He told me he worked in telecom. I said, "That is really interesting, because I have always wanted to work in telecom." I didn't really know what telecom was, but he said, "Great! Call this guy."

For the next several years of my life I was in telecom. I just started trying to climb the corporate ladder. I moved from company to company and ended up at a Fortune 15 company. I was now making ten times what I had been at Abercrombie, and even that was not enough. This relentless chase of money awakened something in me and left me constantly trying to feed this machine. What I had tasted was greed, and it was not good; there was no dollar amount that I would have said was "enough."

I don't know if I would have ever been able to step off that treadmill had God in his mercy not called me into vocational ministry in the unmistakable way he did.

We Care a Lot about Money (& Jesus Did Too)

I tell you all of these specifics, even though I know that sharing the numbers can be a little awkward, because when we talk about the vice of greed, I have lived it. We think about money and accumulating wealth a lot. A 2021 survey from Capital One found that finances are the number one cause of stress (73 percent)—more than politics (59 percent), work (49 percent), and family (46 percent). They also found that younger generations are even more stressed out about finances than older generations, with the majority of Gen Zers (82 percent) and Millennials (81 percent) saying finances are at least somewhat stressful.[1]

Jesus talked about money more than any other single subject (other than the kingdom of God), and he did so out of love for us. Often he would say, "Hey, *this* is what might prevent you from entering the kingdom of God. This is what is going to keep you from realizing your need for a Savior. You will think that you have comfort and security in this life, and you will try to make your home here. You will not long for another kingdom."

Jesus taught about forty parables, and eleven were on the topic of wealth. That means more than 25 percent of the stories Jesus told revolved around our love of money. There is a chance that most of you who are reading this right now have a lot going for you, and you are not heeding his warning. There are days I don't either. We just do not think about it enough. It's like we don't trust him or don't believe him, and we have to learn the lesson for ourselves.

We buy a $4 coffee every day and don't think about it. We just swipe the card, we have the gift card, we earn the points . . . it's just what we do, you know? We get our nails done for $50. We get our hair done for $100, $30, $20—whatever it is. Some of us will mindlessly drop $200 at a department store or shopping online and not even think about it. Right? It's just the air we breathe.

Here's the paradox: on the one hand, you may think that you never think about money, but on the other hand, money so consumes you that not a day goes by when you don't think about it. It truly is in the air we breathe here in America. This leaves us with a mystery we have to solve. Why do we so badly desire something that Jesus so sternly warned us against desiring? Why is generosity so hard for us? Why is it easier to give $1 away when you only have $10 than it is to give $1 million away when you have $10 million? Because money has weight or mass, and mass has gravity. It pulls us off course. And to fight back against the current we're being swept away by is *difficult*.

Money, like most things in life, can be used for incredible good or incredible evil. It all comes down to the posture of your heart. In Paul's first letter to Timothy, he tells him, "For the love of money is a root of all kinds of evil. Some people, eager for money, have wandered from the faith and pierced themselves with many griefs" (6:10). It isn't the money itself that is evil; it is the *love* of money. It all comes down to the condition of your heart. Paul even warns that some people love money so much it has caused them to walk away from the faith!

Chasing after greed and materialism is not a new phenomenon by any means. Scripture repeatedly cautions against a desire for more and more. And no one learned that lesson quite like King Solomon.

The Curse of Wealth

The world has seen incredibly wealthy people throughout history. If you do a quick Google search, you will see the list littered with names you have heard of (and some you haven't). John D. Rockefeller was worth the modern equivalent of $663.4 billion, topping the list for the modern era. But that was a fraction of the net worth of King Solomon. Solomon, the son of King David, had more wealth than he knew what to do with. And it wasn't just that he was sitting on a large pile of cash; Solomon had unending wisdom. He had hundreds of wives and concubines at his beck and call. He had enormous plots of land and every material good you could imagine. Estimates pinpoint his net worth at equivalent to $2.1 trillion. No one has ever come close to him.

In the book of Ecclesiastes, we get a peek at what is essentially a wealthy man's diary entries on the trappings of wealth. As Solomon talks about the futility of wealth, he has all of the authority and all of the credibility to say that. We can sense that he is depressed with just a basic reading of his words. Writing in his last days, he is warning and pleading with us not to make the same mistakes. Time after time, Solomon refers to life "under the sun"—meaning the "here and now" of life on earth. He goes on a diatribe about the curse(s) of wealth in Ecclesiastes 5, saying:

> Whoever loves money never has enough;
>> whoever loves wealth is never satisfied with their
>>> income.
>> This too is meaningless.
>
> As goods increase,
>> so do those who consume them.
> And what benefit are they to the owners
>> except to feast their eyes on them?
>
> The sleep of a laborer is sweet,
>> whether they eat little or much,
> but as for the rich, their abundance
>> permits them no sleep.

I have seen a grievous evil under the sun:

> wealth hoarded to the harm of its owners,
>> or wealth lost through some misfortune,
> so that when they have children
>> there is nothing left for them to inherit.
> Everyone comes naked from their mother's womb,
>> and as everyone comes, so they depart.
> They take nothing from their toil
>> that they can carry in their hands.

This too is a grievous evil:

> As everyone comes, so they depart,
>> and what do they gain,
>>> since they toil for the wind?
> All their days they eat in darkness,
>> with great frustration, affliction and anger. (vv.
>>> 10–17)

Solomon makes several important points in this passage of Scripture. What he is telling us in verse 10 is something we anecdotally see every day: when we love money, "enough" doesn't exist. Much like other desires, when we feed a desire for wealth, it grows. If I feed lust, my lust grows bigger and stronger. If I feed anger, I only become angrier. It is the same with greed. Remember how a $23,000 annual salary was plenty for me? I had all I could ever need with about $2,000 per month, but then somehow $20,000 a month didn't feel like enough. I needed more. I had to feed the machine. Chasing after wealth robs us of satisfaction.

In verse 11, we also see that chasing wealth puts a strain on our relationships. The wealthy can be surrounded by friends, but how do they know if those friendships are real? I think about former pro boxer Floyd "Money" Mayweather. He notoriously has an entourage. He will go into a store, clear it out, and give everything to his entourage. He went into a car dealership once and spent over $1 million on vehicles, just to give to his friends.[2] And he has got to think, when he lies in bed at night, *Are they really my friends? Do they like me for me, or do they like my lake house? Do they like me? Do they love me for who I am, or do they love what I can do for them?* Wealth complicates relationships.

In verse 12, Solomon tells us that wealth can be a curse to sleep. You can have all the money in the world and not be able to rest your mind. You will find yourself lying in bed at night, unable to sleep, all because your thoughts of money keep you awake. All the worries that didn't exist when you had less consume your nights. Now that you have a lot, you wonder, *Is it FDIC insured? What if the market crashes? What's the price of oil per barrel? Should we invest in real estate? Why didn't we do that earlier? We should have bought that thing when it was that price.* Or perhaps that's just me.

Sure, you can buy Ambien and tranquilize yourself. You can pop them every night, not realizing seven years have gone by and you are completely dependent on it. Maybe for you it is a couple of glasses of wine. You are now a machine; you need something to get you up and something to put you down. But you do not have rest. You have been cursed by wealth.

Next, in verses 13–14, Solomon says, "Easy come, easy go." You can bet it all on black and it can vanish. Right? It's all a gamble. The market crashes, planes fly into buildings, pandemics hit, wars are fought . . . who knows what is going to happen? Then, in verses 15–16, Solomon says that wealth can even be a curse in death. Why? Because you can't take it with you, and whatever you leave behind can become an object of war. I have seen it time and time again. Once money becomes involved, family ties can become strained so quickly. You may have all been family before, but now that there is money to be had your siblings are your financial competitors. The scheming begins and the knives come out. (You've seen the movie.) Things can get weird—fast.

Then in verse 17, the word translated "affliction" could most directly translate to English as mental affliction or mental illness. Solomon is warning us that wealth can literally be a curse to your sanity, your ability to think clearly. It is really simple: if you cannot find satisfaction, begin to question your relationships, don't sleep, and life gets complicated—you can lose your mind. You find yourself in this place where you long for simpler times.

I'll ask again, Why do we so desperately desire what Jesus so sternly warned us against? Surely you're like me and have driven by the billboard that shows you what the current lottery payout is. I see that it says $340 million this week and think, *OK, I am just going to go get one ticket; no big deal, right? I could do a lot of good in the world with that money. Hopefully I won't bump into anybody from church there.* Maybe you just get a little scratch off, just for fun. Get a penny, scratch it off, and let's see. You just think, *What if? What if I won the lottery?*

We like to think we would just give it all away and be America's next great philanthropist. *Life would be so much simpler if we just won the lottery.* But we can see that is just not true. *Insider* tracked fourteen lottery winners; here are four quick stories:

- Willie won $3.1 million, but he lost his wife and his kids, was charged for attempted murder, and today is addicted to crack cocaine.
- Michael won $15 million and spent it all on cocaine, prostitutes, and parties. He is currently trying to get his job back with waste management.
- Billy Bob was a preacher. He won $31 million. He bought a lot of things and gave a lot away, but he lost his marriage and committed suicide.
- William won $16 million, was sued by his ex-girlfriend, and had his brother hire a hit man to kill him. In one year, he was $1 million in debt, and today he lives on food stamps valued at $450 a month.[3]

And we think, *Not me! That wouldn't happen to me. I would be different.* Yet time after time we see that wealth curses our sanity.

You Are God's Financial Adviser

What I want you to know is that God has invited all of us to play the role of his financial adviser. He's taken all his money, the cattle on a thousand hills that belong to him, and he's dispersed different amounts to each of us. It's like God is saying to us, *The reason I am giving you this is so you can get it where I want it to go, so make sure you consult me before you take it*—and then we go and spend it all on ourselves. True wisdom comes when we know what God desires for us to do with his money. You're not going to know that apart from spending time with him.

It feels like I am stating the obvious, but even as you're reading this some of you are arguing with me in your heads. You're thinking, *No, no, no; I earned that money. I put in long hours. I did the work. It was a grind.* But who gave you the ability to work? *It was my education. I had a 4.0.* But who gave you the ability to think the way you do so you could go to that school? *It's where I was.* But who made you be born there, when you could have been born in some rural place where you never even saw an automobile? The God who directs all things had you raised up wherever you were raised up. He has given you relationships and opportunities for *him*. There is nothing good that you have that isn't from the Father of heavenly lights, who gives good gifts to his children. Multiple times throughout the New Testament, we are reminded that all good things are from God; he has entrusted them to us.

How can we learn that lesson and forget it so fast? We should pray about every decision we make. *Wait, which ones?* All of them. When you're at a restaurant and deciding what to order, pray about that. Say, "God, do you want me to get steak tonight?" Consult with your small group or your community when you make decisions that involve significant amounts of money (and most decisions involve money). I know this sounds counterintuitive. Americans don't like constraints. We want to do what we want to do when we want to do it. But there is a problem here. When you start doing things, you quickly find yourself in a place where you can't stop doing them. You've fed greed and it's consumed you, and you've found yourself at the top of the ladder—but all by yourself. There is no one there to enjoy it with you, and you're just like Solomon.

I love to travel, more so than most people. When I would go to a hotel room, I would always crank the air down low and leave the lights on. I figured that it wasn't on me and I was going to pay a fixed bill no matter what. Then I went through a biblical worldview course that taught me everything belongs to God. Now, if I believe all things are his, then when I leave the hotel room I'm going to turn the air up to a reasonable setting and I'm going to turn off all the lights. What you do with someone else's resources shows what you *really* believe. For example, you get that per diem from your company and decide to spend it a little bit differently than you would if it were your own money. You think, *Might as well; I'm getting a hundred bucks per day.* But what if you thought, *How can I be a good steward of all resources?* That is a different mindset. If we believe all resources are God's, it shifts our values and shifts the way we spend.

You are not a container for God to store money in; you are a conduit to get it where it needs to go. You are not a pail for him to put his coins in; you are a pipe for him to funnel his resources to where he wants them to land.

The Blessing of Wealth

When we approach financial and material wealth with the right posture, we see that it can also be a blessing—but not just for ourselves. Sure, it will help us meet our needs and allow us to enjoy life. That's God's provision to us. But wealth truly becomes a blessing when we use the resources God has entrusted to us as a way to bless those around us. Solomon speaks to this in Ecclesiastes 5 as well, saying this at the end of the chapter:

> This is what I have observed to be good: that it is appropriate for a person to eat, to drink and to find satisfaction in their toilsome labor under the sun during the few days of life God has given them—for this is their lot. Moreover, when God gives someone wealth and possessions, and the ability to enjoy them, to accept their lot and be happy in their toil—this is a gift of God. They seldom reflect on the days of their life, because God keeps them occupied with gladness of heart. (vv. 18–20)

We can't miss what Solomon is saying here: work hard, earn a good wage, use it, and find enjoyment in what it allows you to do. Understand the lot entrusted to you. Don't worry about somebody else's lot—don't covet what they have. Just live in your lot, bloom where you are planted, and stay in your lane.

This is a beautiful image of contentment. Remember: money is not bad in and of itself. In fact, money can do a lot of good, but it can also easily pull you off course, so the more you have, the more accountability you are going to want, and the more transparency you are going to need. You are also going to need a greater grip upon the gospel. The enemy will use what you perceive as a blessing as a curse in your life to try to pull you out of a right relationship with God by distracting you with the things of this world.

It is great to enjoy material things, just do not make them ultimate. It is not going to go well for you to worship the false gods in this world. This passage says, "God keeps people happy, not their wealth." That's so key to understanding this text; the contentment we long for comes from God. The ability to enjoy wealth is a blessing from God. It is good to enjoy good things. Jesus enjoyed things—always communally. You never really saw Jesus keeping things to himself or packing them into his storage unit like he was on an episode of *Hoarders*. He was always sharing with others and inviting others in, because at the center of his character is generosity. Always sharing, always giving. If he was at a meal, it was communal. To enjoy something is to utilize it. You're not enjoying anything in storage.

Every year I like to grow in discipline by giving up something for an entire year. I have given up sweets, sodas, and caffeine. At the time I'm writing this, I have given up buying things for myself because I am tempted to think I need more. That's why this topic is so difficult for us! The temptation will come today as you're clicking around Amazon or your favorite store sends you an email with a promo code for 20 percent off and free shipping. At that moment, you are going to be tempted to think, *I need more.* Or you're going to walk into the store and think, *I need more. There is something else*

I have got to buy that will make me happy. I want you to say this out loud as the thought enters your mind: "I don't need that. I don't need that." That is right . . . keep saying it. "I don't need that." Keep repeating it when you feel tempted to waste God's resources.

We do not enjoy anything we just spend money on. It will bring only a moment of pleasure or be a coping mechanism when we are by ourselves. We are going to open it up and think, *Oh, that. That is going to look cute in the closet.*

The goal is that we, as Christians, would be the most generous people the world has ever known. But getting there takes practice. We think it would be easy to be generous if we were just rich. But here's an observation: I have never known a generous rich person who wasn't generous when they were poor. Think about the most generous person you know. Have they always been that way? My hunch is that they probably have. I doubt they just turned their generosity switch on once they hit the six-figure club.

Our minds jump to the craziest thoughts, like, *But what if I give it all away? What will happen to me then?* Did you guys hear about the person who gave everything away and starved to death? Me neither. Let's be people who use God's money to do good and share his resources. I'm talking about seeing what you have as his and asking him, "What do you want me to do with this? It's yours."

Here is my challenge to you: make a list of everything God has entrusted you with. Maybe it's money, but it also may be your marriage, your home, your kids, your leadership role within your company, your car . . . make your list exhaustive. Keep it with you for the next week, and then give yourself a letter grade on how you did as a steward of God's resources. Ask God to help you leverage everything you have for the sake of his kingdom. Be a conduit, not a container.

THREE QUESTIONS TO ASK YOURSELF

1. How do you struggle with greed in your life?

2. What's the difference between conduits and containers of God's resources? Which are you more of today, and why?

3. How can you take a step in growing in generosity today?

CHAPTER 4

APATHY & DILIGENCE

When I look back on all of my birthdays, some are more memorable than others. Some just kind of go. When your birthday falls on a Wednesday, it feels more like a Wednesday than a birthday (#welcome toadulting). I remember I really looked forward to my thirtieth birthday. I was excited to move into a new decade—this was going to be the best one yet!

Then I woke up in a world of hurt. My side felt like someone had stabbed me with a rusty blade. I went to the hospital and found out I had a kidney stone. If this was foreshadowing, I suddenly didn't like the outlook for my thirties anymore.

As I was there, they did a CT scan. If you've never had a CT scan, it's where they basically look at your insides, but it's different from an X-ray. Listen, I don't know how that magic works, but they do it. After the scan was over, I went into this other little room to wait for the doctor to come in and discuss the results. You have a lot of time to take stock of your life while waiting at the hospital on your thirtieth birthday! I assumed that when the doctor came in we were going to talk about kidneys and bladders and stones—all that fun stuff. The doctor came into the room and said, "Hey, let's talk about your health." I'm thinking, *Absolutely—I'm in the right place! Let's talk about my health; specifically these kidney stones for sure. They hurt. Have you ever heard it compared to delivering a baby?*

But what he said was, "You're overweight." Whoa. Did this guy just call me fat on my birthday?! I thought, *Well, you know I didn't go calling you names.* I needed clarity. I said, "What does that mean? I don't feel overweight. Why would you say this? And on my birthday?"

Then he said, "Well, it's more on the inside. You have a fatty liver."

Now this felt like he was attacking me. A fatty liver? Is that a medical term? Is that proper? You learned that in med school? That feels like a fourth-grade insult on the playground. "You know you have a fatty liver . . . your mom has a fatty liver . . ." Whatever. I said, "Really? That's where we're going with this? I have a fatty liver."

"Yeah. You're prediabetic. You can get diabetes."

I needed more information. "Prediabetic? So what does that mean?" A million thoughts ran through my head. I felt like I was just sitting there, and this disease was going to jump on me at some point. I was moving toward it. I couldn't know when, but I would just get it. And right now all he could tell me was it's coming my way. Was he giving me a heads-up, like he could see the future? I said, "Doctor, are you telling me I'm a ticking time bomb and I'm about to have diabetes?"

He said, "Not exactly. You really have a choice."

"Well, if I have a choice, I choose not to have diabetes. That would be my choice, final answer."

He clarified, "No, no. If you change some of your habits, you most likely will avoid it. However, if you continue to do what you're doing and stay where you're at in life—if you continue to eat the way you eat and continue to not exercise the way you're not exercising—then yes, you're going to move toward having diabetes. That's going to happen. But if you make some changes to your inputs and outputs, then there's a really good likelihood you will avoid that outcome. You determine your path at this point."

The Fork in the Road

Receiving news like this puts you at a fork in the road. You have a decision to make right now. *You* can determine your path. I don't start there because I want to talk with you about diabetes. This chapter isn't about gluttony; it's about apathy. Apathy is what will happen if you continue to do what you're currently doing. You're at a fork in the road. You *will* drift toward apathy, much like I was drifting toward diabetes. You will be sucked into apathy if you simply continue in the habits you're currently engaged in. But if today you decide to make some changes to your inputs and outputs, you can avoid that outcome. That's the reality we sit in today, as apathy slowly decays the faith of American believers day after day. In fact, a 2022 study from Lifeway Research revealed that three-fourths of pastors believe that apathy is the primary people-dynamic challenge they face in their churches.[1]

A few days after my birthday trip to the hospital, I went home to South Texas to see my parents because my great-uncle had passed away. As I was visiting them, I asked my mom, "How did he die? What caused his death?" She said, "Oh, he had diabetes." "What?" I said. "Oh man, diabetes can kill you?" *He died from that thing I'm evidently about to get? That would have been helpful information to receive from the name-calling doctor.*

Mom said, "Yeah, it's dangerous. It's serious."

See, I think we consider apathy just a cuddly, fluffy struggle. We think, *Oh, yeah, I'm just a little apathetic. This season is really busy. I have lots of stuff going on. I'm not really reading the Word; it's just hard for me right now. My community has to take second place. My small group is hard. I'll be back in the full swing of it soon.* We don't realize that it will kill us and destroy our faith. Just like diabetes, apathy is dangerous and serious.

Apathy is what is going to get you to the end of your life and cause you to look back and realize, *I did nothing of eternal significance. My life was impotent of the power of God. I have nothing to show for myself. No reward stored up in eternity that I can enjoy with Jesus forever and ever and ever and ever. I've completely wasted my faith, or I never really had any.* If these are the thoughts going through your head as you read this chapter, I have great news for you: it doesn't have to be this way.

A Slow Drift

D. A. Carson is one of the leading New Testament scholars of our day. He has done more for modern New Testament scholarship than arguably anyone alive. And he says this, which is the perfect quote as we diagnose the vice of apathy:

> People do not drift toward holiness. Apart from grace-driven effort, people do not gravitate toward godliness, prayer, obedience to Scripture, faith, and delight in the Lord. We drift toward compromise and call it tolerance; we drift toward disobedience and call it freedom; we drift toward superstition and call it faith. We cherish the indiscipline of lost self-control and call it relaxation; we slouch toward prayerlessness and delude ourselves into thinking we have escaped legalism; we slide toward godlessness and convince ourselves we have been liberated.[2]

Think about it this way: When your car is out of alignment, it naturally drifts out of the lane. If you leave your hands off the wheel for too long, you will inevitably wreck your car. Without your effort to do your part, you will end up in a place you do not want to be. You will drift toward apathy naturally. You will not naturally drift toward a more godly, disciplined, holy version of yourself. It will not happen. Which raises the question, What is God's role, and what is our role? We are saved by grace through faith. It is an act of God's kindness and grace to us. The Holy Spirit is sanctifying us, which is also a work of grace, but we are not devoid of responsibility.

You have a role to play. You are to discipline yourself for godliness.

Toward the end of his life, the apostle Paul wrote two letters to a younger man named Timothy. In these letters, Paul tried to communicate all of the important things he believed

Timothy needed to know to be the most effective minister of the gospel he could be. In his first letter, Paul said this:

> Have nothing to do with godless myths and old wives' tales; rather, train yourself to be godly. For physical training is of some value, but godliness has value for all things, holding promise for both the present life and the life to come. (1 Tim. 4:7–8)

Maybe your version of Scripture reads "discipline yourself to be godly." Either way, the point Paul is making is clear: you have an important part to play in your own spiritual growth; it's not going to magically happen on its own. More than watching how you eat, how you work out, or how you care for your physical health in other ways, training for godliness is the most important thing you can do. Discipline means you cannot exclusively do what you feel like and expect to grow in godliness. You will have to do things you don't want to do. Uncomfortable things. Things that stretch you. Things that don't feel right at times. For example, when you are reading the Bible and you say, "Oh, this doesn't make sense to me. I don't understand any of these names or what's going on. It's hard," apathy tells you to just push it aside. Discipline tells you to wake up again the next morning, pour another cup of coffee, grab a commentary, and dive back in.

Understanding Apathy

We need to have a conversation about apathy. Let's start by understanding the etymology of the word. Some of you may be triggered and feel like you are back in your high school

English class, but stick with me. It starts with a prefix, the letter *A*, which means "not/without." *Pathy* comes from *pathos*, which means "suffering" or "passion." So the word *apathy* in its most basic form means "without suffering." We want to skate through life and avoid difficulty, obstacles, and hardships at all costs. Sometimes I feel like an AI experiment: I'm choosing the path of least resistance at every turn. If it's hard to share my faith and easier not to, I choose not to. If it's difficult to read the Bible and easier not to, I choose not to. If it's difficult to fast and easier not to, I choose not to. If it's difficult to be generous but simpler not to, I choose not to. We can just kind of navigate life this way. And it's why we are surrounded by weak Christians—people who go to church weekly (or most weeks, because sometimes it's easier to not go). This is how we got here.

Apathy in any part of your life is often dangerous, because wherever there is apathy, there is a corresponding lack of discipline or diligence. If you are apathetic about your schoolwork, your grades will likely suffer. If you are apathetic about your finances, you're likely going to find yourself over your head in debt. If you're apathetic about your marriage, you and your spouse are going to drift in different directions over time.

Two things are true about spiritual apathy: it is far more prevalent and far more dangerous than we realize. You see, often our suffering forges our passions. I have known so many men and women who have come back from war or some kind of deployment overseas and long to go back there. They want to sit in their platoon again and experience the brotherhood or sisterhood they had there. They went through such a unique shared experience of suffering together. Think about the early church. This is what strengthened believers in the first century. It wasn't the comforts of their new church buildings. It wasn't the lasers, the lights, the smoke machines, the comfortable chairs, or the central heating and cooling. It was the "Run for your life because the authorities want to stomp out Christianity." It was looking back at the end of the day and knowing *we just lost another one.* That's how the message eventually made it to you and why you're reading this book today.

Christianity & MLMs

There are a lot of topics covered in the book of Hebrews, but one in particular is the idea of growing in spiritual maturity. An interesting thing about Hebrews is that we don't definitively know who wrote the letter. A lot of really intelligent, godly scholars disagree. Some believe Apollos wrote it. Some believe Paul wrote it. Others think it was someone else. What we do know is that the Holy Spirit used some person to communicate this message, and that's what's important, right? And we do know why it was written and to whom. It was written to early Jewish Christians who were tempted to return to the tradition that they grew up in.

Now, this is so important for us in the twenty-first century because one of the things that holds us back is we begin to compare church or Christianity to what we've experienced in our upbringing. More often than not, we don't stop to consider that our upbringing might have been flawed. Parts of it may have been a complete and total disgrace to God—unbiblical, even. And I'm not saying we throw it all out; there are parts of it that are good. All of us have this mix of good parts and bad parts. We have to ask ourselves, What of our upbringing was biblically informed, of God, and consistent with the Scriptures? And what of it was of human origin, or traditions that we just hold on to? That's what the original recipients of this letter were struggling with.

Here's what the author of Hebrews says in chapter 5:

> In fact, though by this time you ought to be teachers, you need someone to teach you the elementary truths of God's word all over again. You need milk, not solid food! Anyone who lives on milk, being still an infant, is not acquainted with the teaching about righteousness. But solid food is for the mature, who by constant use have trained themselves to distinguish good from evil. (vv. 12–14)

What we have here is a clear outline of *what should be* the progression of a Christian. You come into the faith as you are saved by grace through faith. Then you grow as a disciple of Jesus. A distinctive of being a disciple is that you begin to pour into others, who then pour into others, who then pour into others, who then pour into others. If you have not seen this before, you have not fully experienced Christianity! Make no mistake about it: this is the Christian process. Anything else is counterfeit to true discipleship.

The best picture I have for you to compare what the Christian life *should* look like is a multilevel (or network) marketing company. Follow me on this: these companies sell products (whatever they might be) that you first benefit from. You think, *Wow, I bought into this, and it had a tremendous impact on me. I want others to benefit too.* Then you use your testimony to offer the product to others, and as you do that, you become an expert on the product and topic. You never knew you were going to be an expert on hair care or cleaning products, but all of a sudden you are because this thing changed your life! That's the best picture I can give you of what should happen in the church. But here is the tragic reality: we get inoculated to it. We are so surrounded by modern Christianity that it's the air we breathe, and our lives aren't really all that changed, so we don't have much of a story to share.

If you look at your life and the life of your atheist neighbor, they are probably shockingly similar. You like the same things. You do the same activities and have similar interests (and, unfortunately, values). The *only* difference is on Sunday you carve out this small block of time for God where you go to a building, sing songs, and read this ancient book and hear someone talk about it. Then you go on about your own atheistic living. And so, when you sit with someone and say things like, "Hey, Jesus changed my life," they are thinking, *No, not really. I don't think he did. You look just like me.*

Here's what we have to understand: that is just not Christianity. Our lives have been changed by Jesus. We grow in his Word, we tell others about Jesus, and we teach them his Word. Where are you in that process, and how long have you been there? The author of Hebrews is fired up and calling people out. They're stuck at the elementary teachings, but by this point they should have been teaching others about the faith. Do you ever feel stuck in your spiritual journey?

Changing Your Diet

How do you fight diabetes? By improving your diet and amount of exercise. How do you fight apathy and complacency? With an improved spiritual diet and amount of exercise. Think about your life for a minute. What are you feasting on, and how are you exercising your faith? What are the inputs coming into your life? What is coming out of your life? Those diagnostic questions will tell you a lot about whether or not you are fighting apathy.

Remember what the author says in verses 12–13: "You need milk, not solid food! Anyone who lives on milk, being still an infant, is not acquainted with the teaching about righteousness."

The baked-in illustration here is of an infant who relies on milk and remains an infant. There is a correlation between what we take in and how we grow, and the author is pointing that out. What we feast on determines how we grow and what we grow into. We know this to be true of our physical lives. Why do we ignore this fact when it comes to our spiritual lives? We fight apathy with a steady diet of God's Word.

I know that there are a lot of hot takes on breastfeeding. (Yeah, we're going there; blame the author of Hebrews if you are uncomfortable.) One of the common debates I've seen is, "Your child is too old. How long are you going to do that?" This has been played out in all kinds of media. In 2012, for example, there was a controversial *TIME* magazine cover of a woman and her three-year-old son nursing while standing next to her. It was jarring to many and stirred up a lot of discussion.

Whatever your opinions are on that cover, I think there is something we can all agree about: there is an age at which all of us would say, "Oh, yeah, that's too old." A twenty-two-year-old coming right to you . . . *Whoa! Whoa! Whoa! Why would you even go there, JP?* Because the author of

Hebrews went there. Those verses about milk aren't talking about Fairlife or Borden. They are really in your face and controversial, very pointed. That is the point, and that's why I went there.

We can all agree that a twenty-two-year-old nursing would be weird (at the least), right? Now think about somebody who's been in the faith for twenty-two years and their diet is still a steady dose of some shallow morning devotional. Now, I'm not dogging morning devotionals; they can be very helpful tools. I am saying that if your diet of the Bible is only a verse here and there, you are spiritually malnourished. This book has a lot of Scripture in it, but it should be a supplement to your Bible reading, not a substitute. If you are choosing between reading this or reading Scripture, ten out of ten times I will tell you to put this book down, break open your Bible, read a chapter or verse, and meditate on it. Journal your thoughts as you go. Get a trusted commentary and read it several times. You're thinking, *Yeah, but it's really hard and I don't understand it.* That's the point! It's in the difficulty, in the suffering, that you are shaped into a disciple.

This has been difficult for me. I am an auditory learner. I love to listen to things, and I love to learn through conversations and debates with intelligent people. Sitting down, opening a book, reading it, and absorbing it has always been challenging. I am one of the few pastors you know who will tell you reading the Bible feels like a chore to me at times. But just because it is difficult doesn't mean I shouldn't do it. That is where I believe my generation and my younger friends miss the mark; once something gets difficult, we bail because we equate difficulty with doing the wrong thing. Just because it's hard doesn't mean it's wrong.

Exercising Your Faith

The other way to grow in your faith is to exercise it—to truly live out what you say you believe. In verse 14 the author says, "But solid food is for the mature, who by constant use have *trained themselves* to distinguish good from evil" (emphasis added). Think about the most spiritually mature friend you have. They live generously, they share their faith constantly and consistently, and they don't gossip about anyone. They only speak words that build others up. They love others well, and they know the Bible. Anytime you ask them a question, they have a verse that applies. Such people have *trained themselves*—diligently and consistently—to distinguish good from evil. They didn't drift there; no one does. They trained for godliness.

Once you change your diet and start feasting on God's Word, you will grow in wisdom as a natural by-product of absorbing more Scripture. You will know what to do in every situation. Psalm 119:11 says, "I have hidden your word in my heart that I might not sin against you."

The promise of this Scripture is that, as we hide God's Word in our hearts, overcoming sin will get easier. Some of you reading this are thinking, *Man, _____ is eating my lunch. I just can't stop it.* Maybe it's porn, alcohol, gossip, nicotine, gambling . . . fill in the blank with whatever sin you are struggling with. Do you want to conquer that sin for good? Start to feast on God's Word. Write it on your heart. That's different from a patch or chewing gum. But it works.

I want to be clear right here: you *cannot* work for your salvation. Your salvation comes to you from God through his Son, Jesus Christ. He died for your sins. God raised him from the dead. He paid the price for you. You are justified by faith and made righteous because of Christ's work. You cannot earn your salvation. But you can work *from* your salvation to make deposits in your eternal savings account. The Bible tells us we can literally store up treasures in heaven through our good deeds on earth. You can work *for* eternal rewards, so that you don't enter heaven smoky and empty-handed, having nothing to show for the decades you were a Christian, saying, "God, I'm here to enjoy forever. Sorry that I didn't actually do any good works on earth in your name." To make the most of eternity, we have to make the most of our opportunities here on earth.

The danger of cohabitating with apathy is that if you do not begin to grow in your faith, one of two things is going to happen at the end of your life. One thing that could happen is you go to hell. You wake up, eternally separated from God, to the realization that you were playing a game and never really had a relationship with him. Or you look back and realize that God, in his grace and mercy, saved you but you did nothing with it. You wasted it. You have nothing to show for it. You embraced a false version of Christianity.

Training with Diligence

Over my years in vocational ministry, I have picked up on so many recurring patterns. A huge part of ministry is simply pattern recognition—a skill we are all taught in elementary school. Here is what I know to be true: if I ask a gathering of one hundred Christians to go to the left side of the room if they feel like they are growing in their relationship with Jesus right now or go to the right side of the room if they don't feel like they are growing, and then I ask the right-side group what their prayer life looks like, how many days a week they spend in God's Word, what their community is like, if they are confessing sin, and if they are using their spiritual gifts, my hunch is they wouldn't be doing any of those things. Maybe some would, but I suspect most would not be.

If I were to survey the left side of the room, those who are growing in their faith, I would see the opposite. I would see men and women who pray like it matters. They would have a time, a place, and a plan for reading God's Word. They would be shaped by the other believers in their lives, and they would be serving all over their local churches. I'm not saying you can simply work your way into a stronger faith, but when you devote yourself to the disciplines of godliness, your faith will grow as a by-product of that.

Here is a reality of life: storms are coming. Trouble is coming. Suffering is coming. And if you have the preexisting condition of apathy, you're not going to make it through. I see this all the time, especially in my younger friends right now, because *deconstruction* is a really big buzzword. It seems synonymous with doubt, and with anger at religious institutions. Many are deconstructing their faith because they got to a stormy place and discovered their faith was built on a shaky foundation. When they faced life's real challenges, the walls caved in. For some the whole house has been torn down, and when it's time to rebuild, they don't know where to start.

In Waco, there is a couple known for fixing up houses. Before they begin to "fix them up," they have to demolish what is there. When it's demo day, they tear down walls, tear out cabinets and fixtures, and even move rooms around. For so many people, when it comes to faith and deconstruction, they get stuck in demo day. Tearing down is the easy part, but they lack the diligence to rebuild. Rebuilding is work. But through diligence, you have the opportunity to build something stronger. If you grow, if you choose suffering now, if you discipline yourself for godliness, your foundation will be strong. When the storms come, you'll withstand them. Your faith will be built up into something that can remain firm through life's biggest challenges.

THREE QUESTIONS TO ASK YOURSELF

1. How do you struggle with apathy in your life?

2. Who is the most spiritually diligent person you know? What stands out to you about their life? Is it something you can emulate?

3. How can you take a step in growing in diligence today?

CHAPTER 5

LUST & SELF-CONTROL

When I was single and living in Dallas (before I was a Christian), my friends and I had a pretty standard weekly routine. Every weekend (meaning Thursday, Friday, and Saturday nights) we would go clubbing (to one club, in particular) pretty close to where we lived. We would meet at somebody's apartment and start with tequila shots. Eventually we would drink a couple of beers. Once we got to the club, we'd move on to the mixed drinks. At 6'7", I needed to be pretty drunk to dance well (or at least what felt like dancing well). It is tough to say how great my dancing really looked.

One night at the club stands out to me, even today. I was out on the floor dancing when I locked eyes with a pretty blonde woman across the room. We started dancing with each other, and as the night went on, the space between us got smaller and smaller. At one point she whispered in my ear, "Come home with me." At this time in my life, that was everything I hoped for. The setting was perfect. The lights were down, the DJ was on point, the drinks were flowing. The night was going according to plan. Around 2:00 a.m., the DJ played "Closing Time" (#classic), and then the lights came on . . . literally.

All of a sudden, I could see everything. There were napkins all over the floor. That musty bar smell became all the more noticeable for some reason. All of the sexy coeds suddenly looked like incoherent zombies, covered in sweat and drinks that they had spilled on themselves earlier that night. And the blonde woman I had been dancing with all night? She now looked desperate and needy. Don't get me wrong—she was beautiful. But there was an emptiness in her eyes I had not noticed before. She continued begging me to come home with her. I told her I thought I should head out with my friends, who were all waiting on me.

Then she did something I did not see coming: she reached into her purse and offered me a couple hundred dollars to come home with her. It was at that moment that a second light switch flipped, one in my head. Her desperation made me hit a new low. This was not fun anymore. It was just sad. I could feel the heaviness in that moment. I said, "I really should be going." It was the first time I'd seen the consequences of someone else's lustful desires catch up to them. It was not cute, and it did not seem harmless. While I did not realize it at the time, this woman was a mirror into my own life during that season.

Understanding Lust

When we talk about lust, particularly within the church, it usually takes on a sexual connotation. Merriam-Webster defines it this way: lust is an intense longing, usually intense or unbridled sexual desire.[1] Can you have lust or intense longing for something other than sex? Sure, but for the context of this chapter we are going to be talking about lust in terms of sexual desire.

I've studied Millennials and Gen Zers up close for the last couple of decades, and I cannot think of a conversation I've had more frequently than with someone trying to figure out how to overcome lust. In my experience, lust plays out in a few different ways. Sometimes these ways follow a linear trajectory; sometimes they do not.

For some people, lust plays out through sexual thoughts and fantasies. That can lead to sexual acts outside of God's intended design for marriage. Maybe this is with a boyfriend or a girlfriend, a friend with benefits (which never ends well), or emotional attachments that start off flirty and then turn physical. Another way is through pornography, which carries a much broader definition than what likely comes to mind. We think of it as only the most explicit corners of the internet, but biblically defined, pornography is fantasizing or thinking explicitly about anyone you are not married to. And pornography leads to masturbation, which is what happens when you are alone with those images or thoughts and do not have the self-control necessary to not fall into temptation. It becomes a seemingly never-ending cycle you cannot break free from.

While I could write a book (and many others have) about each of these issues, we will touch on them only briefly throughout this chapter as we discuss how to overcome lust. Because, as impossible as it may seem to you today, with the help of the Holy Spirit and some practical action steps, you *can* experience the freedom that comes through self-control.

The Thoughts You Are Entertaining

Every action we take, be it good or bad, begins with a thought. Ralph Waldo Emerson, a nineteenth-century poet and essayist, said, "The ancestor of every action is a thought."[2] I cannot think of an area of life where this is more true than lust. No one gives in to sexual temptation, engages in an affair, or pulls up a pornographic website on their phone without first *thinking* about it. When thoughts enter our minds, we really have two choices: we can entertain them, or we can take them captive. We have to learn how to take those thoughts captive, imprison them, and execute them, lest they carry us somewhere wicked and evil.

Is it wrong for you to think about that guy or girl you have a crush on? Well, it depends. If you are thinking she has a nice smile and you would love to take her to coffee, then no. If you are wondering what it would be like to sleep with him, then yes. If we feed those unhealthy thoughts, they are only going to grow more and more layered and more and more difficult to escape. Doing this makes our lives way more difficult.

My friend Jefferson Bethke says that dating with no intent to marry the other person is like shopping with no money. Either you are going to leave frustrated or you are going to take something that does not belong to you. It's the same with the lustful thoughts we allow ourselves to entertain. After enough time, you are going to take action on those thoughts, and it is going to lead you to an unhealthy place.

In 2 Corinthians 10:5, Paul instructs us to "take captive every thought to make it obedient to Christ." These lustful thoughts (the ones that drive you crazy and you think you will never be able to escape) do not have to dominate your thought life. You do not have to dwell on them. You can start practicing taking them captive today. Now, trust me: in the beginning, this is difficult.

If you have never tried to practice this discipline before, you may not be very good at it at first, but Scripture tells you if you are a follower of Jesus and you have the Holy Spirit inside of you, he will help you in this effort to take these lustful, sinful, destructive thoughts captive. This is not a one-and-done kind of deal. This is a grind, and it takes a great deal of time and effort. I have had so many conversations with people who say, "I can't do this," and really what they are saying in most cases (though there are exceptions) is that it was difficult and they gave up too easily.

Here is how to begin: confess sin at the thought level. As soon as you consider the option of sin, confess it. Ask for prayer at the thought level. Before the thought even gives birth to the action, confess it to someone in your small group. This is a step before "Listen, I looked at something I shouldn't have." This is "Listen, I was driving down the road and I really wanted to go to that website or chase that hashtag. I want to tell you that. Would you pray for me?" This is a text message in the moment to the guys or girls in your life who are part of your community, asking them to pray for the thoughts you are having, the strength to not act on them, and a commitment to ask you later about it.

If you get into the habit of confessing sin at the thought level, you will learn how to take those thoughts captive. You can do it. Consistently ask for prayer, because it's a battle of the mind.

The Age-Old Question

Sometimes these lustful thoughts unfortunately do lead to actions. Let me tell you two things: God created marriage, and God created sex. You know how an inventor of a product knows the most about it? Well, God invented sex. In the same way that Steve Jobs thought of the iPhone, God thought of sex. It is not bad, it is not dirty, and it was his idea. But God has a specific plan in mind for sex: that it would happen within the context of marriage. Anything outside of the context of God's intended design is ultimately going to be harmful to us and will fall short of the standard God has set for us.

There is a question I am asked time and time again, both on social media and in person. Everyone wants to know, How far is too far? Everyone is trying to figure out what is in bounds and what is out of bounds. *What can I get away with and still be OK?* I receive over a thousand questions a week, and many are on this topic. "Can we have oral sex?" "Is sexting OK?"

How far can you go without sinning? This is like someone asking, "How close to the edge of a building can I get?" I just start with a question in return: "Well, do you want to jump off?" When you are in a relationship with someone you like and are attracted to, the temptation is going to be there for you to jump—to go all the way. So, for the person who says, "How close to the edge can I get?" my best answer is that if you don't want to jump off, I'd recommend not even getting on the elevator. Since that may be a little too metaphorical for you, let me make it really practical: when your body begins to prepare itself for sex, you've gone too far. Does that help? Need a diagram? I hope not.

God has designed you (and your body) in a very specific way. Sex is his idea, and it's brilliant. He made your body (whether male or female) to function in a particular way, and when it begins to prepare itself for sex, you have gone too far. And that is unloving, both to you and to the other person. It is unkind to make out, to get your body running a hundred miles per hour, and then break away and say, "I've got to go." You should not do that to somebody you care about. Right? Get married and swing from the chandeliers naked; do whatever you want! But outside of marriage, it is always unloving.

I have noticed a few things about Millennials and Gen Zers. They are getting married later, they are getting married less, and their marriages are not lasting. If you are part of those two generations, that is what is happening in your demographic. What are you going to do to change that? People have devalued marriage because this thing (meaning sex) that God has made for marriage, people have said, "No, I'll take it and I'll have it wherever I want." Whether it is sexting, oral sex, foreplay, or one-night stands, anything that is happening outside of God's original design is robbing you of the life that God intended.

I am saying all of this as a man with a significant sexual past. You might say, "Where's the grace in that?" The best news I can give: God has forgiven me of the sins of my past and made me an heir to his kingdom forever and ever and ever and ever. Do my earlier sexual choices impact my marriage today even though I'm forgiven? They absolutely do. Do they impact every single marriage of people who make that choice? They absolutely do. But trust me on this: God's grace can forgive us. The last thing I want to do is heap any shame on your shoulders. I want you to know my story as a way of seeing how God can redeem anyone's past. God's grace can forgive us for eternity, and yet there are consequences to all sin.

No one's ever committed a sin and gotten completely away with it. My best advice to you is to keep that great gift God has given us where it belongs: within the covenant of marriage. That is the only place it's safe. If you are reading this with a heaviness in your heart because you are thinking, *Oh no, I messed up my future marriage long before I even met my spouse*, to you I say: lean in to God's grace. He forgives you, and his Word assures you he's no longer counting your sins against you (2 Cor. 5:19). If he can redeem my story, he can redeem yours too.

The Problems of Porn

As I mentioned earlier, I developed an addiction to pornography when I first got to college. Out of that struggle, my entire life spiraled out of control. Even when I met Monica, my wife, we were both a wreck. We were married in a chapel in front of three hundred of our closest friends and family. Just after the pastor said, "You may kiss your bride," we walked down the aisle smiling ear to ear as everyone cheered. When we got to the foyer of the chapel, I held her in my arms and said this prayer: "God, thank you for allowing me to escape the consequences of my sins of my lust and pornography."

For some reason, I thought that since we'd made it to the finish line of singleness and to this new starting line of marriage, I had a new blank slate and it would only get easier from here. Little did I know that long before I had ever met my wife, my struggles with lust and my addiction to pornography had damaged my marriage.

Now, she and I have experienced healing since then, but lust will damage your marriage long before you even have a prospect. No one in the history of all creation has had a better marriage because of pornography. It hasn't happened. You will not be the first. Let me explain to you why.

Research continually points to the fact that porn is addictive. They could have just asked me instead of funding study after study, but that is beside the point. Pornography is so highly addictive due to the release it causes of extremely high dopamine levels in your brain—some of the highest you can achieve without a substance. Let me hit this home for you: I've done cocaine, I've done ecstasy, I've smoked marijuana, and I drank a lot of alcohol for long seasons of my life. None of those have gripped my heart like pornography.

I would call in sick to work to binge on porn. It just owned me, and I'll tell you why: something secular psychiatrists call *sex glue*.[3] Sex glue is the reality that, during sex, your brain bonds your five senses to your surroundings. When you experience sexual climax, otherwise known as *orgasm* (yup, there it is), your brain creates a synapse or a pathway bonding your five senses to what is around you. Your brain rewires itself to be *addicted* to that feeling.

At its most basic level, pornography is you fantasizing about anyone you are not married to. The reason we all need to talk about this is that today the average age someone is introduced to porn is eleven years old. Read that sentence again. Eleven years old. And 90 percent of kids between ages eight and eighteen have viewed porn. Pornography equates to nearly half of all internet activity. According to a 2020 study, 91.5 percent of men and 60.2 percent of women admitted to viewing pornography in the past month.[4] If we pretend that this is something that is only impacting men or is not destroying the lives of singles and married people inside the church, we are tragically naïve about the scope of the problem.

There are multiple side effects of pornography, one of which is sexual dysfunction. Over the years I have met people who cannot experience sexual release without viewing pornography, because porn is not an addiction to sex—it is an addiction to variety. You have rewired your brain not to bond, as God intended it to, to a spouse. You have trained it to love variety, and as a result monogamy will be very difficult.

Another side effect of porn is an unnatural appetite. When I was addicted to pornography, I had no earthly idea how to love and care for a woman as God would have me love and care for her. I had used women, particularly the two-dimensional kind on the other side of a screen. I didn't know how to care for Monica. Two years into our marriage, as I was trapped in addiction, the wheels fell off.

The third side effect, and perhaps the most devastating, is something called "life numbness," which you and I know more commonly as depression. This is where the normal joys of life are not as joyful. Imagine you are driving on a beautiful fall day: the sun is cracking through the leaves, the birds are chirping in the distance, and there are still waters nearby. A normal Christian would take in a deep breath and give glory to God for his incredible creation. But do you know what that drive is to a porn addict? It is simply not porn. You'll look up from your porn one day and discover you are numb to the everyday joys of life. Everything else seems to have faded to gray, and you cannot enjoy it as you were meant to.

As I mentioned earlier, pornography and masturbation are almost always linked together. It becomes a cycle you are quickly trapped in. Your thoughts pursue the images, then the images push you toward an action. This creates more thoughts, which then push you toward more action. And here is something I have found to be true time and time again, regardless of the sin struggle (but it is particularly true when it comes to lust, pornography, and masturbation): whatever we feed grows. As we feed our lust, our appetite for more only grows. In Philippians 3, as Paul is talking about those who live as enemies of the cross, he says, "Their destiny is destruction, *their god is their stomach*, and their glory is in their shame. Their mind is set on earthly things" (v. 19, emphasis added). When he says, "their god is their stomach," he's saying the enemies of the cross follow their sinful urges. When we are ruled by our desires, we buy into this lie of "one last time" where we think every time we slip up it will be the last time, forever. We operate out of selfishness, not selflessness. And selfishness is the antithesis of the gospel. When you act out *one last time*, you've only fed a desire that will be stronger the next time.

Speaking from my own experience: the effects of an addiction that ended almost two decades ago *still linger*. Today I am still unlearning the content and images I consumed that I thought did not have consequences. There are images stuck in my head from twenty years ago that I could draw for you. They are that specific and explicit in my head. And I truly had no idea that could happen. Nobody told me that split-second decision, that quick moment, was something I would carry into the rest of my life.

In some ways this feels unfair because I'm a believer now. I'm not looking at porn. I'm pursuing purity. I'm in a committed marriage to my wife. But again, viewing pornography is a choice that I made, and I have to live with the consequences of my sin. I believe all sin is equal in that it all separates us from a holy God and it all requires Jesus's death as a payment, but different sins do carry different consequences.

Now, maybe pornography is not your struggle—praise God for that! I do want to caution you, though: make sure your definition is not too narrow. As I mentioned earlier, too often we think of pornography as only being the most extremely sexually explicit websites on the internet. But anything that is causing you to visualize or think explicitly about someone who is not your spouse falls under the biblical scope of *porneia*, the word the apostle Paul often uses in his New Testament letters when describing sexual immorality. Too often we give ourselves permission to indulge in movies that are rated R and have some nudity, or the latest TV show that everyone is watching that has a few sex scenes, as if these ambiguous rules we've set for ourselves equate to the standard of holiness that has been set for us. To be abundantly clear: pornography is sin, without exception. Just because it does not show *everything* does not mean it should make it into your queue of what to watch next or into your Instagram feed. The last thing we need to do is allow these socially acceptable forms of lust to infiltrate our lives instead of treating them as the danger they are.

My story mirrors so many of your stories. Maybe you are right in the thick of it. Whether you are male or female, young or old—if you are reading this and pornography is eating your lunch, here is the most helpful thing I can say to you: healing is out there. And I believe you can be healed.

You Are Carrying Around What's Killing You

For most people (regardless of what particular sin they struggle with), healing begins the same way: removing access to the thing that is destroying their lives. Every time I speak somewhere (be it on a Sunday morning or a Tuesday night or at a conference or retreat), I will hang around at the front of the stage for as long as people want to talk. It is a great time to have conversations, as people are processing what they just heard in the sermon in real time. Because of my openness about my own prior struggles with pornography, I cannot tell you how many times I have had the following conversation:

"Hey, my story is similar to yours."
"Oh, you're addicted to pornography?"
"Yes, I am. Well, I'm struggling with it."
"OK, thank you for sharing that. Let me ask you a couple of questions so I can better understand. How do you access pornography?"
"Uh, through my phone."
"Let me ask you another question. Where's your phone?"
"It's in my pocket."
"Oh, I thought you said you were struggling. You're not struggling; you're carrying your porn around with you. You

have a gateway to millions of explicit images right there in your pocket. You haven't even begun to fight. You haven't even begun to pursue healing."

"So what do you want me to do? Get rid of my phone?"

"That or gouge out your eye. It's up to you. You get to choose. If you want to call me a legalist, let's look at the words of Jesus."

Such an important part of moving toward healing is removing access. Whether it's through filters, software, or swapping out your phone for one without access to the internet, your commitment to getting well is determined by what you are willing (and not willing) to do. In the same way we would all likely counsel a recovering alcoholic to get all of the alcohol out of their home as a first step, you have to commit to cutting off each pipeline that's delivering pornography (or any other content that is causing you to lust).

Jesus pulls no punches about lust in his Sermon on the Mount. Here's what he says:

> You have heard that it was said, "You shall not commit adultery." But I tell you that anyone who looks at a woman lustfully has already committed adultery with her in his heart. If your right eye causes you to stumble, gouge it out and throw it away. It is better for you to lose one part of your body than for your whole body to be thrown into hell. And if your right hand causes you to stumble, cut it off and throw it away. It is better for you to lose one part of your body than for your whole body to go into hell. (Matt. 5:27–30)

It's interesting that he says *hand* when talking about lust. (I think this is an allusion to masturbation.) Jesus is telling us here that lust is not something to play around with. It's not worth it. Even *looking* lustfully at someone who's not your spouse is committing adultery in your heart. He says the sin begins in the mind and the heart, not the actual action. They're one and the same. When you read this, your initial thought might be, *Wow, that's too high of a bar, Jesus. Don't you realize that sex is everywhere?* But Jesus consistently raises the bar for his followers, and sexual purity is no exception.

Why would we carry what is killing us around in our pockets like it's not a big deal? A huge step in the healing process is cutting off access, no matter how drastic the measure seems.

Embracing Self-Control

Here is something else I have found to be true: we will either control our sexual desires or be controlled by them. Living with self-control takes effort and intentionality. It is not just a one-step process; there are multiple action steps we can take. We have already discussed the importance of confessing at the thought level, before we even have an opportunity to take action. Removing access is another important step in the healing process. But what else should we be doing? How else does self-control play out for followers of Jesus?

When Paul sent his first letter to the church at Thessalonica, he was writing to a group of believers living in a very sexually charged place. Likely you and I think we are living in an era of sexual deviance, but we have nothing on Thessalonica back in that day. Adultery, pedophilia, orgies, and homosexuality were extremely common. Things like age of consent did not exist. There were no laws protecting children or slaves from being molested against their will. When I say they were sexually deviant, I mean it.

With that backdrop, let's see what the apostle Paul (inspired by the Holy Spirit) said to the church there:

> It is God's will that you should be sanctified: that you should avoid sexual immorality; that each of you should learn to control your own body in a way that is holy and honorable, not in passionate lust like the pagans, who do not know God; and that in this matter no one should wrong or take advantage of a brother or sister. The Lord will punish all those who commit such sins, as we told you and warned you before. For God did not call us to be impure, but to live a holy life. Therefore, anyone who rejects this instruction does not reject a human being but God, the very God who gives you his Holy Spirit. (1 Thess. 4:3–8)

This passage shows us the dichotomy of lust and self-control (and Paul does not mince words here). We should become sanctified (meaning becoming more dedicated to God and growing in spiritual maturity) and avoid sexual immorality. Paul says the pagans—those who do not know God—act lustfully, but God has called believers to live holy lives instead of being stuck in impurity. If you ignore those instructions, you are ignoring the very God who gives us the Holy Spirit.

Paul talks about self-control a lot. In Titus 2, another letter, he mentions self-control four different times. He tells older men and younger men to be self-controlled, and he tells older women to teach younger women how to display self-control as well. He checks all of the demographic boxes in that one chapter.

In his letter to the church at Galatia, as he is describing the fruit of the Spirit, what does Paul list as one of the ways to see if the Holy Spirit is at work in a believer's life? Self-control. If we are fully pursuing the things of Jesus and living in a manner consistent with his Word, our lives will be marked by self-control.

In 1 Corinthians 6:18, Paul says, "Flee from sexual immorality. All other sins a person commits are outside the body, but whoever sins sexually, sins against their own body." You only flee from things that are dangerous.

When I was dancing with the girl that night at the club, I was doing exactly what I should have been doing. I was a pagan. I did not know any better. Once I became a Christian and the Holy Spirit entered my life, things started to change. Not overnight, but over time as I submitted to the Holy Spirit, I began to experience healing, and self-control did not feel as impossible as it once had.

The easiest way to run *from* something is to run *to* something. If you are running *to* Jesus, you are running *from* sexual immorality. Run hard after Christ. If you are reading this and feel overwhelmed with shame or guilt right now, know this: your shame is not from the Holy Spirit. That is of the enemy. Start by telling your community—bring them into the fight with you. Find a biblically based recovery ministry that will guide you based on what Scripture says. Take it one day at a time and remember: freedom is available to you, and healing is possible.

THREE QUESTIONS TO ASK YOURSELF

1. How do you struggle with lust in your life?

2. Does finding freedom from lust and/or shame feel impossible to you? What Scriptures can you point to today to remind you that freedom is possible?

3. How can you take a step in growing in self-control today?

PART 2

THE MODERN WARS

Everyone has a favorite YouTube video. Mine is called "How to Catch a Baboon." (If you need to pause your reading for a few minutes, just go type that in on YouTube.) However many views it has, I probably account for half of them. If this book hasn't taught you anything else, you are at least going to know where to learn how you, too, can catch a baboon, just in case you ever need a baboon for anything.

The setting is somewhere in the African jungle. This African warrior guy goes to a termite mound, which looks like a large concrete cone. He drills a small hole in the termite mound and puts a little ball-like seed in there. There is a baboon watching him from high up in the trees the whole time. They are curious animals, evidently.

The guy then walks off. The baboon knows this is his moment. He rushes down the tree and toward the termite mound. He puts his hand down in the hole and grabs the seed, but then he can't get his fist out of the hole. You see him begin to panic, screeching and squealing and flipping, about to rip his arm off trying to get free. All he has to do is let go, but the guy comes up calmly and slips a noose around his neck. The baboon is trapped, exactly where the guy wanted him.

I think that is a truthful picture of us. We say, "I want to go all in with Jesus. Just don't make me let go of my relationship, my status, my stuff, the busyness—all of the things that are important to me but are actually a distraction from him. I'm in on Jesus, but don't make me let go of these things." Like a moth to a flame (or a baboon to a termite mound), we find ourselves drawn to the modern comforts, trinkets, and pleasures the world has to offer. We get so assimilated that there is not much in our lives to distinguish us from the nonbelievers around us.

What We Hold On To

One of my favorite Bible stories, which God has used over and over in my life, is the story of the rich young ruler. It is repeated in three of the Gospels (Matthew, Mark, and Luke), so you know it's important. Read the interaction between the young ruler and Jesus:

> As Jesus started on his way, a man ran up to him and fell on his knees before him. "Good teacher," he asked, "what must I do to inherit eternal life?"

"Why do you call me good?" Jesus answered. "No one is good—except God alone. You know the commandments: 'You shall not murder, you shall not commit adultery, you shall not steal, you shall not give false testimony, you shall not defraud, honor your father and mother.'"

"Teacher," he declared, "all these I have kept since I was a boy."

Jesus looked at him and loved him. "One thing you lack," he said. "Go, sell everything you have and give to the poor, and you will have treasure in heaven. Then come, follow me."

At this the man's face fell. He went away sad, because he had great wealth.

Jesus looked around and said to his disciples, "How hard it is for the rich to enter the kingdom of God!"

The disciples were amazed at his words. But Jesus said again, "Children, how hard it is to enter the kingdom of God! It is easier for a camel to go through the eye of a needle than for someone who is rich to enter the kingdom of God."

The disciples were even more amazed, and said to each other, "Who then can be saved?"

Jesus looked at them and said, "With man this is impossible, but not with God; all things are possible with God." (Mark 10:17–27)

Let me tell you a little bit about this rich young ruler. Sometimes, depending on where you have heard this passage taught, he is treated as interchangeable with the Pharisees or the Sadducees (the religious elites) and written off as one of the bad guys. That's missing the point; this guy is not a bad guy. For all the single women out there, this is *the guy* your mother has been nagging you to go out with. He's a good guy. He's not only some kind of successful business mogul but it also appears that he has a deep, abiding relationship with God. He's a catch!

Notice what verse 22 says, after Jesus tells him to go sell everything and follow him: "At this the man's face fell. He went away sad, because he had great wealth." I believe this story is about so much more than a guy with a lot of money who didn't want to give it away. It is about a man who knew what was right and good and true but was so attached to the world and its comforts and everyday trappings—the same ones you and I get sucked into—that he could not fully follow Jesus. To go all in with Jesus, we have to relax our grip and let him pull any idol we are still holding out of our hands.

Modern Pitfalls

We once did a sermon series at our church called "The 7 Deadly Sins of Suburbia." As our sermon planning team sat in a conference room with a whiteboard, we made a list of all of the things in the twenty-first century that distract us and take our eyes off of following Jesus. We filled up the board pretty quickly. Then we started trying to combine them and find some overlap. Even then, the list was eleven or twelve deep. Some were the same ancient struggles we have already discussed, but some were newer.

It highlighted something for me: there are some ways in which following Jesus today looks much like it did two thousand years ago. But also our enemy has gotten crafty and found new, clever ways to distract us and pull us into sin. These newer ways sin has crept in and begun to poison our spiritual lives are something we need to not just be aware of but also know the antidote to. As I thought through the most important modern wars we fight on a daily basis, here are the five I want to address in part 2 of this book:

- Perception Management & Authenticity
- Entitlement & Gratitude
- Busyness & Rest
- Drunkenness & Sobriety
- Cynicism & Optimism

If we can rise above these harmful habits and patterns, we will live in a way that is countercultural and stands out, drastically different from the people around us. And do you know what is amazing about fighting these modern wars? We do it with the ancient, timeless truths of Scripture. While Scripture may not specifically address topics like fifty-hour workweeks, it does give us principles to live by that we can examine and apply to our lives.

Just like the hunter who easily slipped the noose around the baboon's neck, Satan knows exactly how to trap us. The enemy has studied us and has picked up on our patterns. He would love nothing more than to distract us with the bright and shiny objects the world can give us. But there is a better way, one that leads to the full and abundant life Jesus offers us. We just have to be willing to let go and follow him.

CHAPTER 6

PERCEPTION MANAGEMENT & AUTHENTICITY

Most of my adult years were spent living in Dallas, but today I am a pastor in Waco, Texas, not far from the campus of Baylor University (one of the largest Christian universities in the world). This is not the first time I have lived in Waco. I first moved here to get my art degree from the local technical school. The story of God calling me back to Waco is a different book altogether, but let's just say my Waco experiences (pre- and post-Jesus) could not be more different.

When I came for college, I did not know many people in Waco but pretty quickly found some friends to party with, and they were almost all Baylor students. It didn't really matter that we went to different schools; the only thing that mattered was that we all liked to have a good time (which almost always involved a lot of alcohol).

One weekend we did our typical routine: on Saturday night we hung out at the local dive bar near campus and then went to a frat party, and on Sunday we woke up with pounding headaches, smelling like cheap beer. As it was around 11:00, my friend suggested we go to one of the dorm dining halls for brunch (he said he would swipe me in with his ID, and I wasn't about to turn down a free all-you-can-eat brunch).

As I loaded up my tray full of pancakes, eggs, chicken, and waffles, I looked around and noticed something really . . . strange. Almost everyone was dressed up. The girls had on dresses and heels. The guys had on khakis and polo shirts. As I stood there in baggy basketball shorts and an oversized hoodie, I couldn't help but feel like I'd missed the memo. Then it got even stranger: I looked over and saw one of the girls I had flirted with at the bar the night before, and she had on a polka-dot dress and heels. How did she look so put together?

I sat down with my friend and said, "Why do all of these people look like they just had a job interview or went to church?" He said, "Well, some of them did go to church— and some of them just dressed up to come eat so everybody *thinks* they went to church." Wait . . . what? I could not wrap my head around what he was telling me. Why would anyone do that? It made no sense to me. He said, "It's just what some people do here."

Now, up until this point it had not even occurred to me that Baylor was a Christian school. Everybody I was friends with loved to party like I did. I vaguely remembered someone telling me about a required religion class they had to take, and now I was finding out people dressed up for Sunday brunch so others thought they went to church. The dots were all connecting in my head at that moment. (Quick disclaimer: there are plenty of Baylor students authentically following Jesus, but there are also some wearing themselves out trying to look like they follow Jesus.)

My nineteen-year-old, non-believing, hungover self had a thought in that moment that I still identify with now: *That sounds exhausting.* Carefully crafting an image, making sure you are upholding (or look like you are upholding) a certain standard that people have for you, and managing how others perceive you is a terrible hobby. And it is a game we are far more comfortable playing than we realize.

Your Own Brand Manager

With the advent and rise of social media over the last decade, now more than ever you are acting as your own brand man-ager and PR firm. Whether or not we realize it, each of us is cultivating the image we want others to have of us on a daily basis, and it is wearing us out. Maybe the identity you want is "world traveler" or "successful entrepreneur." Maybe it is "loving husband" or "committed wife." Maybe you want to be thought of as a "wise sage" with the perfect picture of your coffee mug and open Bible. With each picture we post or status we update, we run the risk of just playing the game of cultural Christianity that is destroying the church in America today with this veneer of authenticity. It is evil.

For so many of my Millennial friends, this is the root cause of their angst with church today. They grew up listening to their parents arguing in the car on the way to church in their Sunday best, then the second the car was put in park and the doors opened, everyone plastered a smile on their faces and pretended like everything was fine for the next seventy-five minutes. The hypocrisy of it all wore them out, and they reached this point where they said, "If that is church, I want no part of it."

Why do we do this? If we are all exhausted by it, why do we keep running in this hamster wheel of perception management? The explanation is really quite simple. We want to be liked, and all of us, whether or not we want to admit it, are afraid that if people knew the *real* us, they would not like us. So instead, we find ourselves presenting a counterfeit version of ourselves in the hope that the version we present is the "right" one and people will like us, even if it's not *really* us.

Here is the irony of it all: we live inauthentic lives because we want to be liked, but in all actuality the most likable people are the authentic ones! We are drawn to people who are comfortable in their own skin. They have nothing to hide and are the most unashamed, free people we know.

This idea can be traced back to Genesis 2. As God is in the middle of the creation narrative, he creates Adam and then Eve. All is right in the world at this point. Sin has not entered into the equation yet (although it is coming in the very next chapter). They are in the garden of Eden. Everything is perfect! Birds are chirping, the sky is blue, the trees are blooming, and there are Adam and Eve. Notice what it says in Genesis 2:25: "Adam and his wife were both naked, and they felt no shame."

Isn't that an interesting comment for the Holy Spirit to have preserved for all these years? When we think of nakedness, we often first think of shame, but at that exact moment in human history, shame was a completely foreign concept.

As Adam and Eve were fully known, they were completely exposed and were completely shameless. That is something that not a single one of us has ever experienced. Literally none of us have someone who knows *everything* we have thought, *everything* we have said, *everything* we have looked at, and *everything* we have done.

The idea of being completely without shame or guilt can feel impossible to wrap our minds around. We only know a world of trying to control our image and protect ourselves from other people thinking we are more depraved than they already think we are. If we are gut-level honest, many of us fear the opinions of people far more than we fear the opinion of God.

When You Fear the People

King Saul is a fascinating Old Testament character we can learn a great deal from by reading 1 Samuel. If you are unfamiliar with his story, Saul was the first king that Israel (God's people) ever had. Prior to this, they had judges (a cross between a mayor and a military general). As the people of Israel looked around, they said, "Everybody else has a king. We want one of those!" So the people went to Samuel, a priest who served as the middleman between God and Israel. Samuel tried to convince them that God was enough, but Israel wouldn't listen. God then told Samuel to give them what they wanted.

When Samuel went out to search for a king, he found Saul, who just so happened to be everything you would want in an earthly king. He was from a wealthy family, he was handsome, and he was a head taller than everybody else. Every superficial trait Israel wanted in a king, they found in Saul! His reign even started off well as he surrendered to God's Spirit, but soon after his anointing ceremony things started to go south. First Samuel 13 tells us a story about Saul's kingdom coming under attack from the Philistines, their enemy.

You see, the Israelites were vastly outnumbered in this moment, and Saul knew they should make a sacrifice before God. In those days, with a battle looming a priest would make a sacrifice in hopes that God would bless their efforts and make them victorious in battle. But Saul wasn't a priest—he was the king. Kings weren't allowed to offer sacrifices. He needed Samuel to offer the sacrifice, and Samuel told him to wait seven days.

When the seventh day rolled around, Samuel was nowhere to be found, and Saul was done waiting. It was the perfect storm for Saul to compromise, even though he knew the deal. When you're the king of God's people, it's really important to know God's rules. Saul knew he needed a priest to make this sacrifice, but Samuel was late, so he did it on his own. He was so consumed by his standing before others and his desire for people to follow him that he gave in. His followers were nervous (1 Samuel 13:7 even says the troops were "quaking with fear"). He did exactly what he knew to be wrong because he feared the people would revolt.

This was a pattern in Saul's life. Merely two chapters later, after another episode of Saul's disobedience, he told Samuel, "I was afraid of the men and so I gave in to them" (15:24). Saul feared the people more than he feared God, and it cost him everything. God eventually removed his hand from Saul's life and said he would find a new king (who turned out to be King David).

Now, put yourself in Saul's shoes for just a second. You see your people deserting even as you see a huge horde of people intent on killing you headed your direction. What would you have done?

We often put on a façade like we have it all together. We like to project confidence, so we take shortcuts. We do everything we can because we've elevated the approval of people over the approval of God, and we live completely out of balance. Once we're caught up in the game of perception management, it is easy to remove God from the equation altogether.

In his letter to the church in Galatia, the apostle Paul writes this: "Am I now trying to win the approval of human beings, or of God? Or am I trying to please people? If I were still trying to please people, I would not be a servant of Christ" (Gal. 1:10). We can't serve Jesus and serve the opinion of others at the same time. It can't be done. That's exactly what Saul fell prey to. We can't let our fear of other people and our desire for the approval of others dictate our obedience to God.

A (Truly) Deadly Sin

There is another cautionary tale for us about authenticity in the book of Acts. At this point in time, the early church was exploding. People were coming to faith in Jesus, they were living in community, they were sharing their possessions, they were eating together, and they were functioning as a healthy early expression of the church. Right before this story, a man named Joseph (also called Barnabas) sold a field he owned and brought the money to the apostles for them to use for the sake of the church. Enter a duo whom you may not be all that familiar with: Ananias and Sapphira. Let's read their story:

> Now a man named Ananias, together with his wife Sapphira, also sold a piece of property. With his wife's full knowledge he kept back part of the money for himself, but brought the rest and put it at the apostles' feet.
>
> Then Peter said, "Ananias, how is it that Satan has so filled your heart that you have lied to the Holy Spirit and have kept for yourself some of the money you received for the land? Didn't it belong to you before it was sold? And after it was sold, wasn't the money at your disposal? What made you think of doing such a thing? You have not lied just to human beings but to God."
>
> When Ananias heard this, he fell down and died. And great fear seized all who heard what had happened. Then some young men came forward, wrapped up his body, and carried him out and buried him.
>
> About three hours later his wife came in, not knowing what had happened. Peter asked her, "Tell me, is this the price you and Ananias got for the land?"
>
> "Yes," she said, "that is the price."
>
> Peter said to her, "How could you conspire to test the Spirit of the Lord? Listen! The feet of the men who buried your husband are at the door, and they will carry you out also."
>
> At that moment she fell down at his feet and died. Then the young men came in and, finding her dead, carried her out and buried her beside her husband. Great fear seized the whole church and all who heard about these events. (Acts 5:1–11)

Now, as you read that story your first thought is likely, *Wow, that escalated quickly!* Both Ananias and Sapphira dropped dead within three hours of each other . . . but why? Some would tell you their sin was greed, but verse 4 explains they could have used the money any way they wanted, but they lied. Why did they lie?

The sin behind their sin was perception management (or inauthenticity, depending on how you want to label it). They wanted to *appear* as if they were far more holy and righteous than they were. They wanted the same applause and approval they just saw Barnabas receive. There is a very important warning here for us. You see, God really cares about us playing churchy, religious games, and I believe this passage is trying to teach us a couple of things.

One, inauthenticity always harms the people closest to us. Sapphira knew what Ananias did, and it ultimately led to her death. In the early days of my marriage, I worked in business development (a fancier term than sales). Monica would hear me on the phone telling half-truths, trying to spin the conversation in my favor, always trying to land the next deal even if it meant compromising the truth.

When our marriage spiraled downward a couple of years in, it was because she was never getting the real version of me. I was always in salesman mode. I remember driving down the road while we were in the midst of an argument and she said, "Stop trying to sell me on this. Stop trying to persuade me." She could tell I wasn't being authentic, so of course she couldn't trust me.

Two, inauthenticity harms our relationship with God. Verse 4 also says, "You have not lied just to human beings but to God." Here is the thing: if you believe there is a God, then you know he knows the whole truth. If you go to God and don't deal with the whole truth, you are just playing this weird religious game. And you can look up five or ten years down the road and find yourself thinking, *Oh, maybe I don't even believe in God. I've just been playing spiritual games.* You have just been metaphorically (or literally) dressing up and playing a counterfeit version of Christianity.

Like Whitewashed Tombs

Why did God respond to Ananias and Sapphira the way he did? I have a hunch this issue may be one of God's greatest frustrations. Jesus, in the Sermon on the Mount, addressed the playing of religious games a couple of times. He said this in Matthew 6:

> Be careful not to practice your righteousness in front of others to be seen by them. If you do, you will have no reward from your Father in heaven.

> So when you give to the needy, do not announce it with trumpets, as the hypocrites do in the synagogues and on the streets, to be honored by others. Truly I tell you, they have received their reward in full. (vv. 1–2)

> And when you pray, do not be like the hypocrites, for they love to pray standing in the synagogues and on the street corners to be seen by others. Truly I tell you, they have received their reward in full. (v. 5)

> When you fast, do not look somber as the hypocrites do, for they disfigure their faces to show others they are fasting. Truly I tell you, they have received their reward in full. (v. 16)

If your motive is to do something for the appearance of being holy, you have missed the point completely and are grieving the heart of God. But if your motive is to make much of God and to move closer to the heart of God, you are going to grow in maturity and in the likeness of God. But you have to always check your motives. We all do.

Later on in Matthew, Jesus says, "Woe to you, teachers of the law and Pharisees, you hypocrites! You are like white-washed tombs, which look beautiful on the outside but on the inside are full of the bones of the dead and everything unclean" (23:27). This is Jesus speaking! Too often we like to think of nice, cuddly, gentle Jesus. But here Jesus is showing that he has no patience for those who present as holy and righteous on the outside but are decaying on the inside.

One time I was speaking on a panel at a conference with another pastor. I had looked up to him from afar and was very glad to finally get to meet him in the green room before-hand. But as we talked I thought, *Hmm. Something seems off here. This guy seems a lot different offstage than he seems to be onstage.* I know that sounds judgmental, but it felt like discernment from the Holy Spirit.

We went out onstage, and I was so honored to be part of this panel. The discussion was about living in a fishbowl (the idea that in ministry, everyone is always watching you). He was asked a question and responded by saying, "There are some things in life you tell everyone. There are some things that you tell some people. And there are some things that you tell no one." It was like there was a record-scratch in my mind—*Did he just say what I think he said?*

I wanted to be asked another question just so I could bring it back to that statement and ask him to chapter-and-verse that one for me, but another friend of mine onstage beat me to the punch. I was so stunned by his statement because

I just quite simply have never seen that message anywhere in the Scriptures. Your faith may be personal, but it is never meant to be private.

Living in the Light

Fast-forward the tape; that guy was caught having an extramarital affair he was in the midst of while we were up on that stage. That is what happens when you let sin linger and keep it in the dark. When you close off parts of your life to others, however large or small, you are only inviting sin to creep into your life and grow. So what is the solution? How do we rise above perception management and live authentically? We bring everything into the light. And I do mean *everything*.

In Paul's letter to the church at Ephesus, he warns them about letting sin linger in the dark.

> Have nothing to do with the fruitless deeds of darkness, but rather expose them. It is shameful even to mention what the disobedient do in secret. But everything exposed by the light becomes visible—and everything that is illuminated becomes a light. (Eph. 5:11–13)

Paul's encouragement isn't just to stay away from evil. It is to expose evil and bring the darkness to the light, because once you shine that bright spotlight on it, there is no more hiding, no more shame, and the darkness loses its power. You kill darkness with light. That is a theme that is repeated time and time again throughout Scripture. How do you kill inauthenticity? With authenticity.

One night several years ago, I was about to speak and had a pit in my stomach. This wasn't nerves, though. It was guilt and shame. The night before I had been scrolling through Instagram and clicked on an innocent hashtag. Then I clicked on another one knowing it would lead to something sinful. Pretty quickly I saw nudity. By the grace of God, I came to my senses and closed it, but I still should not have clicked, and I had still seen something I should not have gone looking for. Now, about to go onstage in front of a few thousand people, I felt like a fraud.

I walked out on the stage and said, "This is unrelated to the rest of the message, but I want you guys to know what I did because I need to ask for your forgiveness," and I told them the story. I asked for forgiveness, I prayed, and we went on with the night. After I was done preaching, I stood up at the front of the stage to talk to whomever wanted to (which, as I mentioned, is something I do anytime I speak), and I kid you not, I had never seen the line that long before. Person after person, the stories were all the same: "Hey man, me too. Thank you for saying that."

I think the last person left around 1:00 a.m. that night. Here is what I learned: when you are committed to bringing the darkness into the light, it encourages others to do the same thing. Authenticity is contagious in that way. It was not a fun way to start the message. In fact, it was quite humiliating. But God used that moment to spur on authenticity among others, because light always overpowers the darkness.

Some of you who are reading this today have things happening (or that have happened) in your life, and you think you are going to take them to the grave because you do not feel like you can tell anyone. You say, "That's an aspect of my life I'm going to continue to hide from people." I understand that, because there was a time when I was that person. I was that guy who would answer the phone in a different voice, not knowing who was calling. Was it an ex-girlfriend (or an ex-girlfriend's boyfriend)?

Today, I have found incredible freedom that I never believed would be possible because I can say, "Hey, there's nothing in my life that I'm afraid will be found out." It is still amazing to me to think that over the last fifteen years I have reached a place where I can tell the people around me, "You are welcome to explore or inspect any avenue of my life. Anyone who knows me is welcome to look at my phone, my computer, my search history, and my email. You are free to ask anything you need to know."

There is nothing to hide, so be free to walk in the light. First John 1:7–9 says,

> But if we walk in the light, as he is in the light, we have fellowship with one another, and the blood of Jesus, his Son, purifies us from all sin.
>
> If we claim to be without sin, we deceive ourselves and the truth is not in us. If we confess our sins, he is faithful and just and will forgive us our sins and purify us from all unrighteousness.

You don't need to hide any longer. You can walk in the light and find the same freedom I have.

Three Helpful Questions

If I have learned anything about myself, even since becoming a believer, it is this: given to my flesh, if I suppress the Spirit, I am capable of all kinds of terrible things. There is no dog and pony show, there is no act, there is no façade; I am capable of all things (and so are you). I told our church recently that if they knew everything that went through my head in a given week, there's no way they would allow me to preach. But the crazy thing is that even though we all think all kinds of crazy things, we are still allowed to worship a good and holy God who changes our lives.

A part of my protection is a commitment to absolute transparency and authenticity, and this only happens in community with other believers. Here is what that looks like for me. Every Thursday morning, I meet with the guys in my small group at our church, and we work through three questions.

1. "How did you feed your soul?" That is where we can say, "Here are the podcasts I listened to. Here is what I am reading in the Scriptures. Here is this book I'm reading, and this is how God has used it to stir my affections for him in this season."

2. "How have you fed others?" This is a chance to share about the conversations we have had that centered around Jesus. We can share whom we have shared the gospel with and talk about discipleship opportunities we have taken advantage of (or those we have whiffed on).

3. "How have you fed your flesh?" This is an opportunity for honest confession of sin where we can say, "Here is where I've acted in a way that wasn't honoring to God. It was me operating in my flesh." Doing that is humiliating, which produces humility. It is also not fun, but it is life-giving.

I'll just be honest about these three questions: I don't always enjoy answering them. I have asked our church to answer those same three questions in all of our small groups, but not because I think they are super fun to answer. Rather, I think they are a helpful tool for identifying patterns in our lives. It is not the only way but it is an effective one, and it has helped me grow in my relationship with God. Answering those questions on a consistent basis, week in and week out, whether I had a great week or a terrible week, has helped me live my life out loud. It has also helped those closest to me identify patterns in my heart that need to be corrected.

If there is a criticism that's brought against me, it is that I let the people in my life see everything. In my mind, I have forfeited the right to privacy, and I'm committed to that. If I stop confessing sin and stop being transparent, I have told them all to assume I'm hiding something.

When you are trapped in sin, imagine yourself in a cage. The door is locked, and as you look around you see many others in cages too. But because of the gospel, Jesus comes and unlocks the cage. He leaves the door open and invites you to walk out. As you step out of the cage that has held you prisoner, he gives you the key to the cage, which is your story. Every time we share our story and tell what God has saved us from, our sin loses power over us, and others are often freed from their cages. Do not be ashamed of your story. Do not hide it. Use the story God has saved you from, by his kindness, to walk freely out of your cage, and invite others to do the same.

THREE QUESTIONS TO ASK YOURSELF

1. How do you struggle with perception management in your life?

2. Who knows the "real" you? What is the biggest obstacle preventing you from living authentically?

3. How can you take a step in growing in authenticity today?

CHAPTER 7

ENTITLEMENT & GRATITUDE

I often share that I am 6'7" (you should know by now), which I acknowledge is past the threshold of normal height. One thing people say all the time when they come talk to me after I have spoken somewhere is, "Wow, I didn't realize how tall you are," almost like I have been lying this entire time. There are some things that aren't super fun about being this tall. Sure, there are perks. But there are definitely some downsides. Riding in the back seat of 90 percent of cars, for example. If you bolt for the shotgun seat you look like a jerk, so I am always secretly hoping the others in the car will realize they're riding with somebody weird-tall.

I love to travel, but I don't love to fly certain airlines because they don't give enough legroom. Some airlines make their seats for about a max user height of 6'4", which means I've got to just somehow sit awkwardly propped up the entire flight. A couple of years ago I was flying from Seattle to

DFW and was sitting in coach like always. I was about six rows behind the bulkhead, which is the front row of coach. That first row of seats always has a little bit more room, almost like an exit row. When you are my size, that's where you want to be. Sitting there is the tall person equivalent of winning the lottery. When we reached our cruising altitude of thirty thousand feet in the sky, I heard the familiar "ding!" acknowledging they had turned off the seat belt lights and we now had the freedom to move about the cabin. And I saw the whole entire row behind the bulkhead, that front row with the extra legroom, was completely empty—no one was there. This felt like grace, like a gift from the Lord.

I started hatching a plan from my position folded in my tiny seat in the middle of the sky. I decided I would make my way toward the front and talk to the flight attendant. I stood up (so he would see just how tall I was), walked to the front, and said, "Hello, sir. If it's OK with you, I am going to sit in one of these open seats. Nobody's there, you know." He cut me off before I could even get my request out. He said, "Sir, everyone needs to sit in their assigned seat." That didn't make sense to me. We were flying across the country, and *that entire row* was just going to sit empty. I didn't understand why he was so angsty, and I *really* don't like it when things don't make sense to me. But I wasn't about to be one of those unruly passengers who ends up on the news (I was imagining the "Pastor Arrested and Thrown Off Flight" headlines).

I dropped my head and did the walk of shame back to my seat. But get this! No more than ten minutes later another flight attendant came up with someone else, walked him to that empty first row, and said, "Here, have a seat right here. This should give you a little more legroom." This dude was maybe 6'2" on a good day. I was sitting there thinking, *This is not fair! I have been slighted.* I felt like I needed to make sure the other passengers on the flight saw this injustice. I was a victim here! They just did me wrong. And then I started to think about all of the ways I had just been taken advantage of. I was in an unfortunate situation and felt like I was entitled to a logical response. I felt like I was entitled to an explanation. Then I felt like I was entitled to being frustrated because I didn't get what I wanted.

Here is the problem with my logic on that plane: I was in a metal tube full of over one hundred people, going six hundred miles per hour through the sky, carrying me and my luggage over two thousand miles to my home. On this tube I could check my email, text my friends, and watch movies. There were people there to serve me and give me free peanuts and sodas and such, and in that situation, I found something to complain about. I found something to be frustrated about—and it was born out of what I felt entitled to. You see, entitlement is just a more narrow, focused version of the sin of pride. Entitlement is what happens when pride and comfort combine. It's about the things we feel we're owed—what we feel we deserve.

In reality, I was sitting in the seat that I paid for, and I was angry that they didn't give me more than I had paid for.

What We Feel Entitled To

We feel entitled to far more than we think we do: comfort, shelter, health, food, money, safety, a spouse, and so much more on a daily basis. We have set all kinds of expectations, and most of us do not even realize it. So I'm going to tell you a surefire way to know, for the rest of your life, what you feel entitled to: ask yourself, *What do I complain about?*

Whatever you complain about, that's what you feel entitled to. The more you complain, the more entitled you are. These two things go hand in hand. Make a list of everything you have complained about in the last week. If that feels too daunting, make a list of everything you have complained about in the past forty-eight hours. Whatever comes to mind, there is at least *some* level of entitlement involved.

There is no greater window into what people complain about than the NextDoor app. If you don't know what it is, it's pretty entertaining. You can see complaints about dogs barking, churches shooting off fireworks, streetlights that shine too bright, somebody who didn't mow their grass, or somebody who left their trash can out. There's always a bobcat somewhere; everybody sees bobcats. With all these bobcats running wild, you have got to be careful out there! The grocery store is too crowded, the neighborhood has changed too much since they moved there, and their water bill is too high. You want to know what people feel entitled to, just spend a little time on NextDoor.

Some of you are reading this and thinking, *Yeah, but there are some things we should complain about.* We can try to justify it or rationalize it, but let's be honest: everybody who complains feels justified in their complaint. And I'm just telling you, your complaints will point to what you feel entitled to. The challenge with entitlement is that so much of it is just the air we breathe. We are so deep into it and so far from where we should be that if I were to appropriately paint a picture of what needs to change, it would look really daunting.

Every now and then, when I speak at a college or a camp, it will have a ropes course. Most of the ropes courses I've seen include something called the leap of faith. If you haven't seen one before, basically you're harnessed in for your safety and then climb a pole and stand on the top of that pole. As you stand there, you see a bar way out there, in front of you, and you have to jump from where you are standing to that bar. When you're up there, it feels like this daunting task—like you'll never get there. At some point in the leap of faith, as kids do this, they look down and realize just how high up they really are. Their fear comes in, and they say, "I can't do it. I'm gonna climb down."

Today, we're so far from where we need to be. We are so entitled that we are just swimming in a sea of entitlement. It is so much a part of every one of us that when we begin to read the Scriptures, we just glaze over the passages because we think, *That's just too high of a bar. That's too far.* I want to challenge you now to look down, see how far we are and how far we need to go, and commit to jumping to the bar that Jesus calls us to.

Jesus & Entitlement

As I mentioned earlier, Jesus often spoke in parables in order to teach those around him. In Luke 14, we see Jesus going to a Pharisee's house, which is interesting because we think of the Pharisees as the bad guys. They didn't invite Jesus over because he was a fun hang; they invited him over to test him. Because it was the Sabbath day, no work of any sort was allowed. To test Jesus, they brought in a sick man and placed him nearby. They wanted to see if Jesus would heal him (thereby breaking the Sabbath). Jesus, being filled with compassion, healed the man.

Then he began to see people jockeying for position at the table. Back in this day, whenever someone hosted a party, whoever was closest to the host would be in the position of honor. That seat meant something. People would get there early and set their Bible on the chair or lick the knife or something (I'm assuming). They all wanted the favored position. Seeing this, Jesus went into teacher mode.

> When he noticed how the guests picked the places of honor at the table, he told them this parable: "When someone invites you to a wedding feast, do not take the place of honor, for a person more distinguished than you may have been invited. If so, the host who invited both of you will come and say to you, 'Give this person your seat.' Then, humiliated, you will have to take the least important place. But when you are invited, take the lowest place, so that when your host comes, he will say to you, 'Friend, move up to a better place.' Then you will be honored in the presence of all the other guests. For all those who exalt themselves will be humbled, and those who humble themselves will be exalted." (Luke 14:7–11)

What are we supposed to learn from what Jesus is saying here? How should this impact how we live as Christians? You see, entitlement at its most basic level is focusing on what we believe we *deserve*. Entitlement is a hyperawareness of our rights. For the guys in this parable, they felt like they deserved the place of honor, as if it was their right. We talk a lot about rights we are owed, but as Christians you and I are to use whatever God, the sovereign Creator of the universe, has entrusted to us to serve the people around us. That is

Christianity 101. When you are truly living out your faith, you begin to see all of the things you have access to through the lens of *How can I use this to serve others?*

My friend Jim has a better grasp on this than most people I know. I used to have a meeting every Tuesday morning with him and four other people. It was a three-hour meeting and usually ended with the six of us going to lunch. We would all pile into a Tahoe, and one of the six of us—Jim—was seventy-six years old at the time. I would often end up riding shotgun (as already established, I'm weirdly tall), because people sometimes say to me, "Hey, you take the front because you need more legroom." (The legroom can be just as much in the back because that seat moves, but that's just a free fun fact. Don't tell anyone.) I would always try to ask Jim to take the front seat, but by the time I could get to him he'd already be climbing back to the third row. Nobody wants to sit in the third row, but he would always dive for it—every Tuesday.

I got to thinking about this. *Jim knows something I don't know. It's almost like he knows he's going to meet God soon, and he's just storing up treasures in heaven he's going to be able to enjoy forever and ever and ever and ever.* It's uncomfortable in the third row. But Jim understood Philippians 2:3: "Do nothing out of selfish ambition or vain conceit. Rather, in humility value others above yourselves."

Entitled people do not value others above themselves. They don't have time because their world revolves around their own needs and comfort. Want to kill your feeling of entitlement? Make yourself uncomfortable for the sake of others. I don't have a simple or cozy solution for you. But I do know that discomfort kills entitlement. Entitled people are focused on their rights. As the oldest person there, my friend Jim had a right to the front seat, but he used his right to serve others. Back seat Jim wins in the end.

Entitlement Leads to Disappointment

Another thing I have learned about entitlement is that it always leads to disappointment. Always. Every disappointment you have ever experienced comes from your expectations, and entitlement is the most dangerous form of expectation. Think about this: say you work for a great company, and your boss has always been generous. You don't just get a 3 percent raise every year, you get 5 percent. But then the company has a rough year financially, and your boss calls you in and tells you that the company is only going to be able to do 2 percent raises across the board this year. My hunch is, your heart won't swell with gratitude. In fact, you'd probably feel slighted.

Entitlement is the highest platform from which we fall, because while expectations say "I expect," entitlement says "I deserve." *I deserve a promotion, I deserve a marriage, I deserve healthy children.* If it doesn't happen, it's not just a missed expectation; it's an injustice. That is how the people in Jesus's parable felt! They expected to sit near the host, and now they had to sit in the back. They felt entitled to a better spot *and* felt slighted. Entitled people are perpetually frustrated and never thankful for what they have. Remember: you cannot be grateful for what you feel entitled to. This is why entitled people are some of the least grateful people you will ever meet.

Again, we are so far from where we should be. To be transparent, it has been a while since I have thanked God for giving me a roof over my head or a bed to sleep in. Sometimes my paycheck will hit the bank, and I won't even stop to say,

"Thank you, God, for a job I love that allows me to provide for my family." I just expect the money will magically be there on the first and fifteenth of the month. My refrigerator has enough food for weeks in it. If we were trapped in our house for a month, we would live. I never think to thank God for that—not one time.

Could you imagine trying to describe your life to your great-great-great-great-great-grandfather? Say he magically appeared and has a few minutes to ask you what life is like. There you are; you hand him a cup of tea as you're sitting around the fire, and he says: "How do you get water? How far do you have to walk?"

"You know, I just walk to the kitchen, or if I want to go to the bathroom, I guess I could do that."

"Hold on. The water comes into your home?"

"Yeah."

"How do you make it hot?"

"We have sinks and stuff. Turn on the hot faucet, you get hot water."

"How do you get it hot? Do you have to set a fire in your house?"

"Yeah, we have a fireplace. It's really just for looks, though. Sometimes we like to sit by it when it's cold, but we don't really need a fire. We have a hot water heater, you know."

"Oh, so does the hot water heater keep you warm when it's cold?"

"No, not really. It just makes the water hot. We have central air and heat. We have a thermostat."

"What's a thermostat?"

"It's this thing on the wall that sets what temperature it should be inside. I control mine from my phone."

"Wait, what? So you keep your food cold with the thermostat?"

"No, we have this other box. It's called a refrigerator, and we put food in there. It's different because it would be too uncomfortable if it was that cold in the home."

"Do you keep your horses warm with the thermostat?"

"No, we're not really horse people."

"Donkeys?"

"Not really our thing. We have cars."

"What's a car?"

"It's a motorized vehicle that takes us places."

"So where do you keep the car?"

"In a garage."

"What's a garage?"

"It is kind of like a house, but for the car."

"Wait. You have a house for your car?"

Think about how crazy this sounds! You and I have so much to be thankful for. But can I tell you why we're not thankful? Our abundance has killed our gratitude.

You don't need to feel bad about having a lot. Every good thing comes from God. You do need to repent for not being grateful. If God has entrusted you with a lot, that is awesome—don't ever stop being grateful! You can ask him to take anything that you're not grateful for, because you cannot be grateful for what you feel entitled to.

Grateful People Win

I want to let you in on a little secret I've discovered after almost two decades of vocational ministry: grateful people always win. And to take it one step further: entitled people always lose (and often with an abundance of things, no less). They can't be grateful for anything. They always expect more. Grateful people, on the other hand, live entitlement-free. They are able to celebrate the wins of others without feeling like they are losing. These are the people who hold a team or a staff together because they are just grateful to be along for the ride (without concern for where their seat is). Their perspective has changed, and they have an eternal view in mind instead of worrying about the here and now.

You see, the gospel kills entitlement. If we have a right understanding of what Jesus did for us, we understand that by our actions we are deserving of hell and eternal separation from God. That is what we are *entitled* to. But because of the sacrifice of Jesus on our behalf, we receive something we do not deserve and are not entitled to. The gospel is the story of the King of the Universe, the Creator of all things, becoming a servant and humbling himself even to the point of death on a cross.

One time I went on a trip to Rwanda, where we went to train some pastors and government officials on conflict resolution. We taught for four days at a "conference center," which was really an open-air courtyard. On day one we could see the major differences between the government officials and the pastors. The officials arrived each morning in tailored suits and shiny shoes or elaborate, flowing dresses. The pastors came barefoot, with holes in oversized suits cinched together by belts. As the week went on, two individuals in particular stuck out to me.

One of the women always wore a really bright, colorful, flowing dress with a train, and she always had some sort of elaborate hat on too. I could not quite figure out who she was or why she was so important, but it was clear to everyone in the room that she was someone special. She had someone save her a front-row seat each morning. Her hats were made of feathers and towered so high they obstructed the view for everyone behind her. When it was hot (and it always was), she had people fan her. She was just a diva. I don't know how else to say it. Whoever she was, whatever her title, her position had clearly gone to her head a little bit.

The other person I noticed was a pastor who was just a servant; he overflowed with joy and was so kind. I watched him serving everyone around him every day. He let everyone else sit down first, then took the least desirable seat (directly behind the lady with the feathery hat). Even though his view was obstructed each day, he diligently paid attention and scribbled notes. His posture told you everything you needed to know about him.

On the last day we did an illustration on stewardship, teaching the principle that we are to get God's money where he wants it to go. We drew one person's name completely at random to win two envelopes. All they knew was that one envelope contained more than a week's wages. Everyone knew there was a lot of money at stake, even though they didn't know how much. We drew the name, and truly just according to the sovereignty of God, it was the feathery hat lady's name. So we gave her the two envelopes.

Everyone applauded. This lady milked it; she was the perfect drawing winner. She stood up, she bowed, she soaked in the applause (all for a chance drawing). She opened the first envelope, and it was the money. It was more than they expected. Everybody was going crazy, and she was just smiling and glowing like, "Yes, I did it!" Then she opened the second envelope. It said, "Give it to the person behind you." Never had I seen an illustration work more perfectly! None of us could believe it. The pastor tried not to take the money (of course) and just lowered his head. She was in shock that she had to give it to that guy. It all went according to God's plan.

Listen, I don't know what the reckoning will look like, but I believe with everything in me that there are people building palaces on earth who will hand them to the servants of God in eternity. In that moment in Rwanda, I learned a lesson I will never forget. Ultimately in the end, God is in charge of who gets what, forever and ever and ever and ever. He says things like, "The last will be first" (Matt. 20:16), and we act like it is an abstract metaphor. But I believe God means what he says, and grateful people win.

Thanksgiving & Christmas

There is no shortage of modern psychological research on the impact of gratitude on our physical and mental well-being. This is an area of life where scientific research is catching up with what Scripture has been telling us for thousands of years. Scholars from Harvard to UC Berkeley and everywhere in between have put the idea of gratitude under the microscope to see how it impacts us as people.

One easy way to evaluate yourself is to think about how you approach Thanksgiving and Christmas. In America, we set aside these two days per year to slow down and be grateful. One falls the day before the biggest shopping weekend of the year (Black Friday to Cyber Monday), and the other is centered around exchanging gifts. We have let the meanings of these holidays get hijacked somewhere along the way.

But what if, instead, we lived each day as if it were Thanksgiving and Christmas? What if our lives were centered around giving thanks to God for all he has done for us and expressing gratitude for our Savior? There are twenty-four psalms about giving thanks or gratitude (so roughly one out of every six psalms). Gratitude should be a regular occurrence, or else we will end up entitled. Here is what I have found to be helpful: each morning I write down five things I am grateful for that day. It is a discipline I force myself to practice in the same way I need to read my Bible or pray through my prayer cards (see *A Praying Life* for more on those).

What I am thankful for is not always earth-shattering—and I think that may be the point. Sometimes it's a theological truth or my wife or a coworker or the roof over my head. Sometimes it's a great meal or laughter with friends. And if you do the math, five items a day for a year adds up to almost two thousand things to be grateful for *each year*. I need that practice, because without it I will drift into entitlement.

The other thing I am doing (as I am writing this) is abstaining from buying things for myself for this calendar year. As I mentioned earlier, I try to give up something annually as a discipline, and this year I felt a conviction about how quick I was to treat myself to a little retail therapy (especially if I found a good deal). Even a few weeks into the year, this started to expose something in my heart about what I felt entitled to.

If we're not careful, we will develop a hole in our gospel. Even the disciples, who most closely walked with Jesus during his time on earth, missed it. Do you know what question they asked Jesus most often? It wasn't how he did the whole water-into-wine thing. It wasn't how raising Lazarus from the dead worked. They most frequently asked *which of them was the greatest.* They asked who would sit at Jesus's right hand in glory. They missed the whole part about leveraging everything given to them to serve those around them. Because that's what Jesus did. If we're not careful, we will cut that uncomfortable part out of our Bibles and live a self-serving existence here on earth.

These two practices are shaping me into a more grateful, less entitled version of myself. If you are looking for a place to start, I highly recommend trying these for yourself.

THREE QUESTIONS TO ASK YOURSELF

1. How do you struggle with entitlement in your life?

2. Take five to ten minutes and make a list of all the things you have complained about in the past week. That will give you a glimpse into what you feel entitled to. What stands out to you from this exercise?

3. How can you take a step in growing in gratitude today?

CHAPTER 8

BUSYNESS & REST

I don't know about you, but I have to operate every day with an awareness of my calendar. All day every day, my calendar is updating me and telling me when my next thing is, how far away it is, what time I need to start driving there, and any other details I need to know. I'm only able to focus on the next thing, then the next thing, then the next thing. I have learned that I work best that way, which always makes January a bit of a struggle. I am not sure what your workplace is like, but for me the beginning of the calendar year symbolizes a busy season. The new year begins, and I feel like I hit the ground running every time. Each January, I find myself in retreat mode. We have a staff retreat, a leadership team retreat, an elders retreat, and then a sermon planning retreat where we map out the entire year. And don't let that word *retreat* fool you, because nobody's retreating; it's all just planning out the upcoming year.

My Mondays start with a management meeting in which I gather with the people who report directly to me to game-plan for the week ahead and debrief from the week past. It's the time of week I feel like an air traffic controller, and I love it. One Monday morning in January I was prepping for that management meeting. I arrived at one of my favorite local coffee shops a bit early so I could think a little beforehand, and I was pondering how I wanted to be a better encourager to our team in this new year. I knew that good leaders are great encouragers, and I was resolved to devote more time to brainstorming how I could encourage those around me. I began thinking through each person whom I was about to meet with and the words of encouragement I wanted to speak over them. But you know how it goes. In the middle of that exercise, I began to think about all the things we needed to do.

I thought about all of the things from the previous Sunday we needed to talk about. Not to mention the fact that we had another Sunday coming up around the corner. The thoughts just flooded my brain as I sat on the beat-up leather couch in the corner of the coffee shop. Then I had this thought: *Busyness is the enemy of encouragement.* Think about it—it makes sense, right? It felt divinely inspired. I wrote it down and waited for the team to get there.

Once everyone arrived, I started us off by saying, "Hey, this is a thought I had this morning that I want to share with you guys: 'Busyness is the enemy of encouragement.'" I expected them to grab their phones and tweet out my Monday morning wisdom, but they didn't. In fact, someone said, "Hey, think about how many things you could put in that blank."

"What do you mean?" I asked.

"Well, busyness is the enemy of _____. You could put so many words there." And so, we did that exercise. We went around and began to fill that blank with different words. Think about how you would finish the thought: Busyness is the enemy of _____.

The truth is, we could fill in that blank with any number of words. Busyness is the enemy of happiness, because it steals joy from us when we're so occupied doing other things. Busyness is the enemy of relationships, because we can't go deep with other people when we don't have time to prioritize them. Busyness is the enemy of compassion, because we don't allow ourselves the opportunity to stop and serve those around us. Think about yourself. What is busyness robbing you of?

A Permissible Sin

I love what my friend said. It shows how inoculated we are to busyness. It is one of those sins that we have let creep in and become so mainstream that we don't even see it as a big deal—and all the while it is robbing us of the lives Jesus intended us to live. We accept it as a given, as if we have no choice but to live this way. Even worse, we wear busyness as a badge of honor, like it elevates our importance.

This is one of those issues that seems to impact each generation too. College students, young adults, singles, newlyweds, families, empty nesters . . . everyone seems to willingly jump aboard the busyness bandwagon. All of us have a limited amount of time, and we all have the same amount of time. And life is really full. The Pokluda family has three kids in school, playing sports, and that would be enough to occupy most of our weeknights right there. Factor in work, extended family, our small group, friends to see, sermons to write, and meetings to be at, and the hours in the week disappear really quickly!

But don't for a second think I'm trying to sound important, because I know you have all your own stuff to do. I know, as I am describing my life, that you are thinking about yours. *Yeah, practices, assignments, work, studying for the LSAT, family, fixing up the house . . .* We all have some sort of working to-do list flooding our minds right now. Some of us are hyperventilating, and I get it. I get it. We are all too busy. But here's a grim reality that becomes more and more clear to me with each passing year: I don't like myself when I'm busy. I become a version of myself that I don't much care for.

And I have a hunch that you also would not like me very much when I am busy, and I probably would not like you very much when you are busy either. When we are moving fast, we don't love people well. When I am busy, what falls off first is kindness. Then my ability to focus wanes. I may physically be with you, but my mind is writing a sermon or figuring out where I need to be next, and I am not being a good follower of Jesus with you at that moment. I also lose empathy when I am busy. I don't have time to care.

But what I lose most is my peace and joy. I have noticed that I take on a victim mentality. *Don't you get it? I'm busy! I'm really busy. You just need to understand that I'm busy!* And I turn outward and begin to lash out at others because I am a victim of my own busyness. It's not like I have cancer or some incurable disease. I just didn't manage my time well. I just didn't say no to some things. I got myself in this situation that I'm now projecting onto you.

Andy Crouch, a Christian author, says this about busyness:

> I have to say "no" to requests many, many times a day. Almost always people are understanding. They often say, "I know you are very busy." The truth is I am NOT very busy. I try not to be busy at all. But in order for that to be true, I have to say "no" many, many times a day.[1]

We have to discipline ourselves to say no to all sorts of things—even good things—because busyness is a tool the enemy will use to kill our intimacy with Jesus.

A Tale of Two Reactions

Luke's Gospel account teaches us a lot about busyness. Luke was a physician with a keen eye for detail. In Luke 10, he writes about Jesus sending the seventy-two disciples. Then he writes about Jesus telling the parable of the good Samaritan. As Jesus sends out the disciples, he's showing them that they are going to need margin to do his work. If you think about it, the good Samaritan is also really a story about margin, right? The priest goes by, the Levite goes by—there's a man hurt and lying on the side of the road, but they don't have time to care for him. Then the Samaritan comes and saves the day by caring for the injured person. After that, we read the story of Mary and Martha. I believe Luke is trying to get a point across by arranging all of these stories in this manner.

> As Jesus and his disciples were on their way, he came to a village where a woman named Martha opened her home to

him. She had a sister called Mary, who sat at the Lord's feet listening to what he said. But Martha was distracted by all the preparations that had to be made. She came to him and asked, "Lord, don't you care that my sister has left me to do the work by myself? Tell her to help me!"

"Martha, Martha," the Lord answered, "you are worried and upset about many things, but few things are needed—or indeed only one. Mary has chosen what is better, and it will not be taken away from her." (vv. 38–42)

Let's just talk about what is going on so we don't miss what is happening here. Jesus comes to town and is hanging with his friends. Martha is in the mix. Her Enneagram is most likely 1 wing 2. Martha is proactive, she's a perfectionist, she's the homeowner. They're at Martha's house, and she's ballin' out of control. (I'm pretty sure that's what the Greek says: "Ballin' out of control.") My point is, Martha has all her ducks in a row.

And then there is Mary. Mary's an Enneagram 4: artsy, more creative, kind of freethinking, maybe a little flippant or flighty. Mary is a little more unpredictable. She's hanging at Martha's house because Martha has it all together. And to the Marthas of the world, the Marys are extra annoying, because it seems like they get a free pass. And so, when Martha comes to Jesus and says, "Tell her, Jesus," and he responds, "She's done what is better," we can all feel her. *Wait, what?*

I know everyone likes to talk about Jesus's kindness and compassion, but Jesus just put Martha in her place. Imagine the perfectionist 1 who has it all together saying, "Hey, I'm trying to keep all of these plates spinning; would you just tell my sister to help?" Now picture Jesus saying, "Well, she's actually doing a better thing than what you are doing." We should feel the weight of that. "Martha was distracted by all the preparations that had to be made" (v. 40). *Distracted*. With Jesus right in front of her, Martha's mind was elsewhere.

Busyness Robs You of Focus

Let me tell you what this looks like at my house. Imagine it's dinnertime. We have prepared a meal; it's on the table. Monica's there, the kids are there, and we're all taking our seats. Then it is time to pray before the meal, and the kids are fighting over who gets to pray. This exact moment is the perfect snapshot of what you'd hope your pastor's dining room scene would look like. All is right in the world; we're about to eat and break bread together.

Ding! Ding!

It's my phone. Maybe it's a DM, a text message, an email—I'm not sure what it is, but somebody needs me. "Green beans, pass the—Hey, I'll be right back, I'm just gonna check my phone real quick." I go check my phone. It's a smartphone, obviously. It's a brilliant phone, because this little device in my hand suddenly has all the worries of the world just flooding in. And there it is, there's the message. "Yeah! Glad I took that one, because it was important. Someone needed me. . . .

But now I'm back with you guys!" But I'm not back—I'm distracted. My head is now in a thousand different places because that one little "Ding!" took precedence over the people at the table with me.

How many times do we do this to the people around us? Maybe it is in a meeting where we put our phones on the conference table just in case something takes precedence over the meeting. We do it to our small groups. We do it at dinner to our friends and family. We leave ourselves open to distraction, and it robs us of our ability to be fully present with the people closest to us. Distraction is far more dangerous to our walk with Jesus than we believe it is.

Think about this: What are the things that only you can do? What are you uniquely qualified to do? I have a few answers for you. First and foremost, you are in charge of growing your relationship with Jesus. In the church world, I can't tell you how many times I've heard, "I just don't feel like I'm growing. I'm sitting in my small group; it just doesn't feel like they're feeding me." Nobody else is in charge of you eating! You are responsible for your own spiritual growth. Depending on your stage of life, I may be able to add a couple of other things to your list. No one else is able to be the mother or father to your children. No one else is able to be the husband or wife to your spouse. These are the jobs you are uniquely qualified to do, and if something is robbing your focus from living out those aspects of your calling, then it needs to be bumped off your plate. Those extraneous things—even the good ones—cannot take priority over your relationship with Jesus, your role as a parent, or your role as a spouse.

Busyness Robs You of Empathy

Pay attention to what Martha says in verse 40. "She came to him and asked, 'Lord, don't you care that my sister has left me to do the work by myself?'" She's saying, "Jesus, don't you care about me? Tell her to help me!" Martha is the victim here. Mary's against her, Jesus is against her, no one is for her, and she's trying to carry everything all by herself. She's blaming everyone else for her problems, because busyness breeds a victim mentality and makes you a master utilitarian. Everyone's either for you or against you. If they can help you accomplish everything on your to-do list, great! If they can't, then they're wasting your time. Before too long, you begin to see people through that lens. "If you're not helping me get this done, then you're not for me." "Tell her to help me! Are you not on my side?" You can become uninterested in what others have going on because you see the tasks on your plate as more important than what others are doing.

Think about how self-absorbed that sounds. "I can't slow down to focus on your needs because I have my own needs." Empathy takes time, and we run at such a frenetic pace that there is *no* extra time. None. And this is why I think the story of Mary and Martha shows up right next to the parable of the good Samaritan. The priest is off to the races with religious tasks to accomplish. The Levite has got stuff to do and places to be. The Samaritan basically trips over the person, clears his day, and ministers to him because he *got it*.

We are slaves to the idea of "It might not get done!" Well, it might not get done. And if "it" (whatever it is) does not get done, but you serve the people around you well, then that is ultimately going to be OK. If our capacity to serve those around us is hindered by our own productivity, we have bought into the lie that our busyness is a badge of honor connected to our importance. Let me tell you something clearly: "I'm busy" does not, in any way, mean "I'm important."

Somewhere in your subconscious you have nurtured this idea that if people knew how busy you were, they would find you to be important. But here is what you might really mean when you say things like "I'm busy":

- "I manage my time poorly."
- "I'm __ years old and haven't learned how to say no."
- "I'm a slave to what others think of me, and I don't want to disappoint anyone."
- "I'm on the verge of a mental breakdown because I just cannot do this anymore."

You may be saying any one of those things, but you certainly are not saying that you are more important than anyone else.

Busyness Robs You of Peace & Joy

Now look again at what Jesus says to Martha in verse 41: "Martha, Martha . . . you are worried and upset about many things." This is what Jesus notices about Martha. Busyness has stolen her peace and her joy. Jesus, the literal Son of God, is in her presence, and she is worried and upset because she let busyness win.

What if it all doesn't get done? What if? Think about all of the what-ifs in your present reality. What if you don't finish the assignment? What if the house doesn't get cleaned? What if the kids don't get picked up from practice on time?

What if? The greatest thing you can do with that question is answer it. It really removes the teeth of the enemy. What if the house doesn't get cleaned? Then you have a messy house.

What if the kids don't get picked up from practice on time? Then they sit there another fifteen minutes. Maybe everybody gets in their car and talks about what an awful parent you are; maybe somebody calls CPS and tells them, "Man, you're not gonna believe this. They were fifteen minutes late to the pickup line today."

Christmastime rolls around, and what if the ornaments don't get hung or the stockings don't get done? Everybody's coming over and there you are, putting ornaments on the tree. What if you don't finish? They could make you stand on the hearth in front of the fireplace and take turns making fun of you, telling you how pathetic you are. I mean, I imagine that's going to be a pretty incredible story. Probably front page of your local paper. Some journalist is going to say, "Everybody was coming to her house. She knew it. She was putting ornaments on the tree—but she didn't finish. How pathetic is she?"

Think about what we have done. How did we get here, so far from where we should be? We have prioritized so many wrong things, and we have let the enemy steal our joy in the process.

The Problem Isn't Margin

Life is inherently busy, so if you are in a place where being busy frustrates you, you are really setting yourself up for a life of frustration. Ask anyone a life stage or two ahead of you—it just gets busier and busier for a long time. In most cases, you will accumulate more and more responsibilities as life goes on. If you find yourself resistant to the reality of responsibilities, you're setting yourself up for trouble.

The world has countless solutions to this universal problem. If you go to any bookstore, chain or local, new or used, you will find it has a self-help section. Row after row full of so many books that are going to give you resources to live your best life. In fact, there's a word you'll continually trip over. If you say, "Well, my schedule is really full," they'll say, "Well, you just need some _____." If you say, "Man, I can't come up for air. We're always doing something," they'll say, "Well, you just need to build _____ into your schedule." Do you know what word goes into the blank? I said it at the beginning of the chapter. *Margin.* "You just need *margin.* Just create some *margin.* All you need is *margin.* The solution to your busyness is *margin!*" It is treated as a one-size-fits-all solution to your busyness problem.

Now, let me tell you this: margin is not bad, and they're not wrong in the sense that when life throws you a curveball, margin can be really helpful. When you have a clear day and a problem comes your way, it's extremely helpful to be able to shift all of your time and energy to solving that problem. In that situation, margin is helpful. We've already established that Jesus teaches us that margin is necessary to do his work well through the story of the good Samaritan.

The problem is, building in a lifetime of margin is not sustainable, because things are always going to be coming after your calendar. I want to propose a different word that I think is biblical, one this passage about Mary and Martha is pointing to: *prioritization.* We have to consistently evaluate what our priorities are and what falls into which order. You have to figure out, right now, what your non-negotiable things are. What will you not trade? That way when the curveballs come (and they will), you'll be able to easily figure out what deserves which percentage of your attention and focus. You might think that's idealistic, but I'm just telling you that people have been practicing prioritization for a really long time, and those are the people who are able to get it done. Martin Luther, one of the theological giants responsible for the Protestant Reformation, once said this: "I have so much to do today that I'm going to need to spend three hours in prayer in order to be able to get it all done."[2]

There are a couple of things I have found to be true over the years, all at the same time. One, everyone has a different capacity, meaning different people are able to carry different loads of weight. Two, everyone has the same amount of time in a day. And three, anything that you put as a priority over learning from Jesus is a bad trade. I think sometimes people want to believe this in theory, but when it is time to put it into practice they do not have the faith to *believe* it.

I see parents fail to prioritize Jesus all the time. Maybe you want to see your kids go to an Ivy League school, so you cut corners on discipling them in the way of Jesus Christ for the sake of a better standardized test score—and that is a disastrously bad trade. They will lay their Harvard diploma at the feet of Satan. Or you want your children to play professional sports—they're going to be one-in-thousands great, have an amazing career, and make seven figures, and you're all going to gather around the TV to watch them in the big game. You'll get there because, though the tournaments fell on Sunday, you know that "Jesus is most important, but we've got to do this. We don't control the schedule! We have to get you better and get you on that travel team." It's a bad trade, and one hundred years from now, once you're dead and have gone to be with Jesus, you are going to realize what a terrible trade you made.

You can say Jesus is most important to you, but people learn what is really most important to you by what you say no to.

A Battle for Our Souls

There is a battle going on for your soul right now. I believe the enemy would love nothing more than for you to live a distracted, busy, burned-out life. We talk about burnout a lot in the church, but I think we need to reframe how we think about it. We often think burnout happens when we are doing too much, but I believe it happens when we are doing the wrong things *by our own strength*. The goal is not that we would simply have empty calendars; it is that we would be focused on the tasks God has given us, with the right motivations.

Here is a question I have found to be helpful: What makes *you* love God more? The beauty of it is that there is no right or wrong answer; everyone can answer it differently. Some of us might say reading the Bible or spending time in nature, or reading the Bible while in nature. Maybe for you it is discussing theology with a trusted friend over a cup of coffee. Maybe you like to turn on your favorite worship album and take a bubble bath. I don't care what your "thing" is, but I do want you to figure out your answer to that question. Once we know the answer, it reframes *rest* in our minds. Instead of merely vegging out or bingeing the newest Netflix show, we find rest becomes an opportunity to do the things that stir our affection for Jesus. Doing the things that make us love God more grows our love for and confidence in him.

King David talks about the rest that comes from our souls finding confidence in God in Psalm 62:

> Truly my soul finds rest in God;
>> my salvation comes from him.
> Truly he is my rock and my salvation;
>> he is my fortress, I will never be shaken.
>
> How long will you assault me?
>> Would all of you throw me down—
>>> this leaning wall, this tottering fence?
> Surely they intend to topple me
>> from my lofty place;
>> they take delight in lies.
> With their mouths they bless,
>> but in their hearts they curse.
>
> Yes, my soul, find rest in God;
>> my hope comes from him.
> Truly he is my rock and my salvation;
>> he is my fortress, I will not be shaken.
> My salvation and my honor depend on God;
>> he is my mighty rock, my refuge.
> Trust in him at all times, you people;
>> pour out your hearts to him,
>> for God is our refuge.
>
> Surely the lowborn are but a breath,
>> the highborn are but a lie.
> If weighed on a balance, they are nothing;
>> together they are only a breath.
> Do not trust in extortion
>> or put vain hope in stolen goods;
> though your riches increase,
>> do not set your heart on them.

One thing God has spoken,
　　two things I have heard:
"Power belongs to you, God,
　　and with you, Lord, is unfailing love";
and, "You reward everyone
　　according to what they have done."

In the opening line of this psalm, David states, "My soul finds rest in God." When we hear the word *rest*, our minds often jump straight to physical rest. What David is describing here is a bit more complex than that. It's rest that comes from confidence in both who God is and what he will do. Why is David's life marked by confidence in God? Because he has seen God move. When our souls have confidence in God, it is easier for us to exhale.

At the beginning of this psalm, David makes declarative statements about God's character and his nature. He calls God both his fortress and his salvation (v. 2). A few verses later he describes God as his refuge (vv. 7–8). *Refuge* isn't a word we use a lot, but rarely do we seek refuge when things are going well. And too often, when our lives are in turmoil, we seek refuge in whatever will help us escape it or numb the pain. Instead, David gives us a template for how to call out the pain and difficulties of life for what they are, while also bringing them before God and saying, "Here's what I'm feeling, and in spite of all of these things that are beyond my control, you are my refuge." He then wraps up the psalm by expressing his confidence in what God would continue to do in the future, because he knows God's track record throughout his own life.

This is the lesson I keep learning in my life too. When we discipline ourselves and devote ourselves to the things of

God, our souls find rest (and restoration) in a way we never thought possible. When we get busy, we get self-reliant and self-dependent. And when we get self-dependent, the first thing we squeeze out is the spiritual disciplines. And here is my public service announcement for every one of us: we will not grow as followers of Jesus without them. It is never going to happen. I am here to tell you that you will not be the first person in the history of history to grow as a follower of Jesus without practicing discipline. It's never occurred, and it will not with you.

Yoked to Jesus

Each Friday, I field a bunch of random questions on Instagram about following Jesus. One week, someone asked me, "Have you ever thought about leaving Christianity because it's so exhausting?" I was taken aback by the question, and in my response I said, "Are you sure that's Christianity?" Because here is what I read in Matthew 11:

> Come to me, all you who are weary and burdened, and I will give you rest. Take my yoke upon you and learn from me, for I am gentle and humble in heart, and you will find rest for your souls. For my yoke is easy and my burden is light. (vv. 28–30)

It is easy for Jesus's message to be lost on us here because few of us are farmers and even fewer of us have used a yoke (side note—there are some great YouTube videos explaining how yokes work, but I know this is the chapter about not wasting time). The people Jesus was talking to definitely would have understood what he was saying. A yoke is much different from a harness; a harness is used to multiply horsepower from the animals. But a yoke, in Jesus's culture, was used as a tool to train young animals how to do their job and be useful to their master. This distinction is so important. You would attach the yoke (made of wood) around the necks of an older animal and a younger animal. As the older animal turned left, the younger would turn left as well. If the older animal turned right, the younger did too. Everything the older, more experienced animal did, the younger one would do too. By submitting to the older animal, the younger was able to learn how to do what was required of it. Jesus invites us to come to him and learn from him.

A helpful (albeit slightly hokey) acronym I once heard for *busy* was "Being Under Satan's Yoke." Satan will use busyness to rob us of the lives Jesus intends for us to live. The idea of taking Jesus's yoke upon our lives, however, should inspire us to hit the ground running each morning. Jesus is inviting us, with all of our burdens and our baggage and our weary souls, to find rest in him and to learn from him. He did the heavy lifting on the cross.

Through him you gain eternal life with God in paradise. As you look forward to that day, live with that in mind. Breathe deeply. Start your day knowing that God wins in the end. Make time to do nothing other than reflect on that reality.

THREE QUESTIONS TO ASK YOURSELF

1. How do you struggle with busyness in your life?

2. What's the difference between margin and prioritization? What would it look like for you to aim for prioritization instead of more margin?

3. How can you take a step toward achieving rest today?

CHAPTER 9

DRUNKENNESS & SOBRIETY

I grew up on a farm. I am not a farm kind of guy. Most of my childhood Saturdays were spent with my dad, making a thirty-minute drive even farther out into the country, where he kept cattle. When we got there, we would go from property to property with the exact same routine: I opened the gates so he could feed the cows. For him, the cows weren't pets; they were his livelihood. For me, they were just something that stole my Saturdays. I hated every minute of it. While my other friends were playing, I was helping my dad feed the cows. My job was to open gates, and his job was to count the cows and feed them.

On our way home, my dad would usually stop at this country gas station, which was my opportunity to buy some candy. It was an unfair payment for a wasted Saturday, in my opinion. On one Saturday in particular, when I was fifteen, my dad couldn't go, so he sent my older brother in his place.

As usual, I opened the gates. My brother fed and counted the cattle. On the way home, we stopped at the same gas station. He went in, and I stayed in Dad's truck. He came back with two cans of beer. "Want one?" he asked.

I wasn't quite sure how to answer, so in an effort to decline yet keep even a sliver of my older brother's respect, I said, "Uh . . . I don't know. I don't think I like beer." "Suit yourself," he said, and cracked open his can and put the other one in the center cupholder.

"I guess I'll give it another shot," I said. I picked it up and tried to smoothly crack it open as he did. I took my first drink of beer ever, and as it turned out, I was right: I didn't like beer. Was that how it was supposed to taste? I wanted to spit it out all over the dash. It tasted so bitter, almost rotten. I wondered what was wrong with my taste buds, since it seemed that so many adults really liked it. It didn't have the sweet taste of Coke or Dr Pepper that I enjoyed. *Why would anyone choose beer over soft drinks?* I wondered. Then I learned why. After I got about half of that can in me, I felt different—relaxed and a little silly. My brother and I didn't normally talk much, but we were talking now. Or at least I was. And then a very strange thing happened: the beer started to taste better.

That wasn't my last beer. By the time I moved into my senior year of high school, my friends and I were always looking for the next keg party. That's what we would do in our small town. We would meet in a pasture, off the road where no one could see us, and we would drink. Sometimes in the winter months we would build a fire. Guys with sound systems in their cars would provide the music. If there was no fire, headlights and the moon would provide the light, and we would just drink. If I'm honest (and I told you I would be), I have really fond memories of those times. It was a lot of fun, even though it doesn't sound like it now. Imagine the conversation:

"What do you want to do?"

"I've got it!"

"What?"

"Let's go circle up in a pasture, stand around, and drink until we want to throw up."

I get it—that doesn't sound like fun. But it was.

I think it was fun because we didn't feel accountable for what we did. If we made out with someone, well, we couldn't be held responsible. It was like some other spirit was in control. Turns out, that's why they call liquor stores places that sell "wine and spirits." Because it *is* another spirit in control. While you are absolutely responsible for everything you do, you are not in control. The Bible says, "Do not get drunk on wine, which leads to debauchery. Instead, be filled with the Spirit" (Eph. 5:18). This Scripture presents a dichotomy for believers: either we are controlled by the Holy Spirit, or we are controlled by some other spirit. The spirit of tequila, rosé, bourbon, IPA, or something else.

I've done many things I regret under the control of those other spirits. I have had pregnancy scares, had knives pulled on me, had guns pulled on me, gotten in fights, ended up in handcuffs a couple of times, and even spent the night in jail once, all because of those other spirits and my submission to them. That list doesn't even include the many times I prayed to die while hugging some nasty toilet, covered in my own vomit, with only a raging headache to look forward to the next morning. I'm not sure the "fun" was ever worth that.

I wish it stopped at alcohol. After that day with my brother, I sought escape through many substances. Listen, I am not in any way blaming him or that single experience. I'm confident it is my own rebellion that led me to pursue drinking and drugs in my young adult years. I first got high in high school, when I was partying with my friend's sister. The THC from marijuana made me feel like I was dreaming. It seemed to relax me while simultaneously making me feel paranoid. I realize that doesn't make sense, but it did.

There was a season of my life when I smoked every day. This is interesting, because I never *really* liked it. Everyone else seemed to like it, so I just felt like I should too. It left me hungry and just feeling like I was wasting my life. In college I tried ecstasy (also known as MDMA or "molly") for the first time. It just made me feel good—and that's it. There was an intense "good" feeling in the moment. Afterward, I was left in a state of depression for a couple of days. I felt like my brain had no serotonin left, and with it went my joy. It was also in college that I tried coke. Not the sugary drink but the snorting kind. That felt like a serious next step for some reason, but I learned I really liked the feeling of up more than the feeling of down. It gave me lots of energy and made me feel invincible. The morning after, I woke up wanting more, and that scared me. I remember thinking, *People give their whole life to this.*

Identifying the Problem

I realize these are strange things for a pastor to confess in the final pages of his book. My point in doing so is not for shock value but to help you. Maybe you've never snorted cocaine, and maybe you've never even smoked weed. Good! But I am still surprised by how many people who claim to be Christians are OK with getting drunk. It's like we hide behind the question, Where's the line, really? And if we don't have a clear answer to that question, we feel free to cross it. I want to be clear: the Bible condemns getting drunk. But I don't think it condemns alcohol altogether, as some pastors teach.

I do believe that Jesus's first miracle was turning water into alcoholic wine in John 2. I do believe Jesus, the One we follow, sipped wine at the Last Supper with his disciples. The line we are not to cross is getting drunk. Let me help you define this: when it feels better to sway than to stand still, you're most likely intoxicated. When you feel your body relax, and when you begin to feel anything as an effect of the alcohol (whether you call it "a buzz," "tipsy," or "drunk"), something else is beginning to take control, and it is not the Holy Spirit.

Even after all my years of following Jesus, I am surprised by how many so-called Christians will say things like "I need a glass of wine." That is language that implies they are using a substance for an effect. This is what Scripture warns us against. The Holy Spirit calls us all to be alert and sober-minded (1 Pet. 1:13; 4:7; 5:8). That's the line to remember: remain sober-minded.

When you're headed to a wedding and you're wondering if there's an open bar, you might have a problem. If you're looking forward to the next time you can unwind with a drink, you might have a problem. If that's you, I want to encourage you to get help. If you're arguing with me while you read this, and you're wondering why smoking weed is wrong (I'm asked that often), it's because THC makes you high almost instantly. High or drunk is the other side of the spectrum from sober. Sobriety is what Scripture calls us to. As believers in Jesus Christ, we must remain sober.

Alcohol is a drug, and drugs are addictive. I've counseled thousands of young adults. None of them said, "I want to be an alcoholic when I grow up," but many of them did just that. Alcoholism runs in my family. I have seen it take *everything* from people. The enemy does not want us to be under the control of the Holy Spirit. He does everything he can to keep us enslaved to any substance. I am asked weekly, "How do I stop drinking?" or "How do I stop smoking weed?" I have met with people who have traded everything good in their life to take one more hit of crystal meth, heroin, or some other drug.

I'm not fearmongering here. In truth this issue is a lot scarier than I'm making it sound. If you have a problem, allow this to be the sign you're looking for to get help. Alcohol can be an excuse to do stupid things. Alcohol can be your escape from a hard day. The problem is you don't sleep well (this has been proven), you wake up groggy and maybe hungover, and all your problems are still there. This is why so often alcoholism leads to depression. Again, please get help if you need it.

Living Wisely

While sober thinking is the call of Scripture, it is not the only warning about alcohol. First, you should never drink if it is against the law to do so. This means if you're underage or are somewhere it is not allowed, you should not drink. Romans 13 and other Scriptures are clear on this. Many Christians know not to drink around those who struggle with alcohol.

This is a tough one, because if you're at a bar, there's a good chance you're surrounded by people who struggle with alcohol. Be sure and be very thoughtful here. I've talked to many alcoholics who have been "OK" with people drinking around them. However, all of them would prefer they didn't. As a follower of Jesus, we are called to forfeit our freedoms for the good of others. Romans 14:13–23 calls us not to cause someone else to stumble into temptation because of our uses of freedom.

It is honoring to the Lord for you to be considerate in this. Similarly, 1 Corinthians 8 calls us not to drink around those who believe it is wrong to do so. Tragically, many Christians never even consider this. We are tempted to be annoyed if someone seems legalistic. However, Scripture calls us to set aside our freedom so that others are not tempted to judge us by our actions. Lastly, Proverbs 31:4 is a warning for kings not to drink. Again, I think this hits on the importance of making judgment calls with a sober mind. In short form, here are the Bible's rules around alcohol:

1. Don't drink if you're underage or it's illegal (Rom. 13).
2. Don't drink if you're addicted (1 Cor. 6:12).
3. Don't drink if you're tempted to get drunk (Eph. 5:18; 1 Pet. 1:13).
4. Don't drink around those who struggle with alcohol (Rom. 14:13–23).
5. Don't drink around those who believe it's wrong (1 Cor. 8).
6. Don't drink if you're in a position to make important decisions (Prov. 31:4).

We are called to "set [our] minds on things above" (Col. 3:2) and to "not conform to the pattern of this world, but be transformed by the renewing of [our] mind[s]" (Rom. 12:2). The battle is for our minds. The Spirit wants control of our minds, and Satan wants to keep our minds from being controlled by the Spirit. Intoxication is a key strategy of his. When we are beaten down by the world, we often try to escape it. Deep prayer and Scripture meditation are your best ammo to endure the stresses of this world. Meditation might require more work than taking a shot or shotgunning a beer, but it is also healthier and more God-honoring, and there's no hangover—only joy.

Sin Robs You of Creativity

When I graduated from college and headed to Dallas, I moved five times while remaining within two miles of the club district. That's where my heart was. Alcohol was such an important part of my life. I was a weekend warrior, someone who lived for the weekends, during which I'd make blurred memories of random hookups, bar fights, and friends doing stupid things, like the time my buddy jumped on the hood of a Porsche (PS: if that was your car, I'm so sorry!).

That Porsche was parked outside a club. It was the same club I was at when someone invited me to church. They picked me up the next day, and I went and experienced the grace and forgiveness of Jesus Christ. I came to this place where I thought, *If this gospel is true—if I'm going to die and be somewhere forever—I should live for that instead.* I would just go to the bar every weekend. What was "so fun" sounds pretty ridiculous right now, looking back. Sin robs you of creativity, and my friends and I were a prime example of that. We would do the same things over and over, with the same empty results.

There have been lots of campaigns against drugs. Through the years, I have seen many different commercials warning of the dangers of drug use. One of my favorites was a more honest approach. As I recall, the scene was of some friends sitting on the couch smoking weed. They scoffed at the warnings, and the first guy said something like, "We smoked weed, and we didn't start doing harder drugs." The next guy said, "Yeah, we didn't get in a wreck or hurt anyone." Another chimed in, "We didn't get arrested or go to jail." Then the first guy said, "We didn't do anything." Then, in a moment of clarity, they realize their whole lives have passed them by—and they didn't do anything. Their "harmless" weed had robbed them of ambition. Their greatest desire was just to sit on the couch and get high. They never grew up. They wasted their lives.

When God saves you, he calls you to a purpose. There are "good works" he has prepared in advance for you to do (Eph. 2:10). God does not want you to waste your life. He does not desire that you escape this world by being high; rather, he calls you to use your gifts to redeem this world. He wants you to make the most of every opportunity. In Ephesians 5:16, just before exhorting believers not to get drunk, Paul says, "[Make] the most of every opportunity." He then goes on to say, "Do not get drunk on wine, which leads to debauchery. Instead, be filled with the Spirit" (v. 18).

Intoxication helps you make the *least* of every opportunity. You quite literally waste your life. You make a bunch of memories you can't even remember clearly. Many people have told me, "Drinking isn't that big of a deal." Great! If it's not that big of a deal, then just don't do it. If you do drink, do it to the glory of God. Live as 1 Corinthians 10:31 instructs us to do: "Whether you eat or drink or whatever you do, do it all for the glory of God."

My father was an extraordinary man. My best comparison for him is like a modern-day John Wayne, but fun. He was always the life of the party. He was charismatic and could work a room like no one else. He was always the president of something, whether it was the Lion's Club, the country club, the booster club, or some other club. People looked to him to lead. He was a hard worker. He never seemed to mind giving up his Saturday in exchange for work, and he always took me with him because he valued time with me.

My rebellion was not his fault but my own. My parents did all they could to point me to Jesus—a foundation I will always be thankful for. When I was in my early twenties, my dad got vertigo really bad. He was dizzy all the time and seemed so miserable. The doctors couldn't find the cause or provide a cure, so he started to self-medicate with alcohol. I never saw my dad drunk until the day he met Monica (now my wife). He and my mom had gone to the beach for vacation, and Monica and I met them down there for the big introduction. He stood up to give her a hug and fell back down in his chair. Honestly, I was too confused to be embarrassed. After that day, my father was drunk most nights. He was not an angry drunk. He would just pass out in his chair. It didn't have a major effect on me, except when we would drive six hours to see him. We'd get there at night, and he'd be sitting in his chair with a bourbon and water. He was always extra jovial. He'd ask a bunch of questions, only to ask those same questions the next day. This was always frustrating to me. Not because I'd have to answer the questions again but because I knew he didn't remember my answers because he'd been drinking.

In 2018 my dad had a heart attack. It didn't kill him, but while in the hospital, he went through alcohol withdrawal. When the ambulance took him from our small-town hospital to a bigger hospital an hour and a half away, he hallucinated the entire trip. He told me he saw us running behind him, chasing the ambulance. The withdrawal almost killed him, and it scared him. The doctor told him if he ever drank again, he would die. I went home and taped pictures of our family, with all his grandkids, in the two cabinets where he kept alcohol. The Lord kindly gave us a little over a year with my dad sober. Our kids loved their "Pops." He was generous, adventurous, and always had the answers.

In 2020 he died shortly after he'd started drinking again. I guess the doctor was right, though it's difficult to know exactly what killed him. (So you have all of the information, he did have COVID at the time. He'd also smoked for two decades and then exchanged smoking for drinking for the next two decades. He had a lot of health issues.) I'd give anything to open another gate for my dad on a Saturday. They weren't wasted days at all. Those Saturdays are now some of my fondest memories.

Alcohol has never made anyone healthier. Smoking anything has never made anyone a better follower of Jesus. At the beginning of this book, I told you that you can't stop a bad habit; you can only replace it with a different habit. I'd encourage you to replace drunkenness, or any kind of intoxication, with sober thinking. "Then you will be able to test and approve what God's will is—his good, pleasing and perfect will" (Rom. 12:2).

THREE QUESTIONS TO ASK YOURSELF

1. How do you struggle with drunkenness in your life?

2. Where have you drawn the line when it comes to alcohol (or any other substance)? Which of the six rules listed in this chapter resonates with you the most?

3. How can you take a step in growing in sobriety today?

CHAPTER 10

CYNICISM & OPTIMISM

As complex and complicated as the world is today, it is still really easy to divide people into two different camps. Even as you are reading this, you know there are two kinds of people. There are cat people and there are dog people. This is just a basic fact of the human experience. But you can divide people over more than just their correct (dog) or incorrect (cat) choice of a favorite animal.

Let's think about fast food. There are In-N-Out Burger people and there are Whataburger people. All of the "Texas forever" people love them some Whataburger. If you are reading this from your home in California, you are probably an In-N-Out person. Good for you, California.

But it doesn't just stop there! There *are* two kinds of people. It all comes down to how you pronounce one simple word: GIF. It is a debate that tears families apart. Here's the deal: I know some of you are thinking, *But the acronym and the word starts with a* G, *like* gift *with no* T. But the inventor of the acronym says that it is indeed pronounced "jif," with a *J* sound. So it's solved now. It's *GIF* with a *J* sound.

There are indeed two kinds of people. There are those of you who go zero inbox every single day of your life. You cannot go to sleep if you have an unread or undeleted email. Those little bubbles drive you crazy. You have to clear them right away. Then there are those of you with 3,596 emails (or in my case, 77,281). If I haven't emailed you back, I'm going to get to it.

All of these examples are kind of fun. They don't matter, but there *are* indeed two kinds of people, and I believe with everything in me that this one *really* matters. There are those of you who see the glass as half full, and there are those of you who see the glass as half empty. The way you view the world is through that lens. But so what? I know what you are thinking. *I'm just a little pessimistic by nature. It isn't a big deal. I'm just a realist, and everyone else is living in a fantasy world. I'm a critical thinker.* But it *does* matter, and I am convinced it matters to God too.

Let me say this up front: it is easy to understand how we got to such a cynical place. The explosion of smartphones, the rise of social media, and an addiction to the 24/7 news cycle all played a role in getting us to this point. You and I are bombarded with negative news stories, divisive issues, and polarizing debates. We feel pressured into taking sides (because admitting we are uninformed doesn't really seem like an option), and all of this negativity has an effect on our brains and how we process information. We rush to our phones to escape the world, and there we are met with even more negativity. We have become trapped in a cycle of cynicism without even realizing it.

Debbie Downer

I know you may be skeptical right now, if you are bent toward cynicism. I promise you that this is not me telling you to just think happier thoughts and everything will be great. That is not a very compelling vision. I simply do not believe it is God's desire or hope for you to live a glass-half-empty kind of life.

In 2003 *Saturday Night Live* introduced a new character: Debbie Downer. The premise was quite simple. Debbie (played by Rachel Dratch) would appear in different social settings, such as a dinner at Disney World or a party, and would interrupt conversations with negative declarations, stories, or facts (often involving the plight of cats, proving my earlier point). Throughout Debbie's total of nine appearances, she was accompanied by a sad trombone sound effect after each comment she made. Without fail, the cast around her would break character and laugh each time she was on.

What made Debbie funny wasn't just the trombone or her facial expressions. I think Debbie was funny because she was relatable. Sadly, we all know somebody like her. We all know that person who without fail will point out the negative in a sea of good things happening. They can always tell you why something is a bad idea before you have even tried it. They never expect the best-case scenario to play out; they always default to the worst. To put it succinctly, these people are a drain on whatever room they are in. And Christians are not meant to live that way.

Before God called me into ministry, as I mentioned earlier, I worked in corporate America. In one job, I had a supervisor I'll call Ken. Ken was a real-life Debbie Downer. He had been beaten up by the world, and it really affected him. He carried that with him everywhere he went (particularly work). As we would sit in meetings, Ken would rattle off projections, sales, and other important numbers, and it *always* felt like we were losing. It *always* felt like our entire team was about to get laid off. It *always* felt like the situation was doom-and-gloom. That was just life working for Ken.

Every time my cell phone would ring, and I would see that it was Ken, my heart would sink a little bit. I would think, *OK, it's been a good run, but today is the day I get laid off.* And that was an exhausting way to live. In the beginning of my working relationship with Ken, it just felt like he was always having a bad day. But over time, Ken's jaded view of the world began to impact me (and the rest of our team). That's what cynicism does; it clouds your perspective to the point you can't see the world as it really is, and it's contagious.

Living as the Older Brother

Let's be honest: it is easier to live with a critical spirit. It is easier to default to cynicism. Resolving to view the world through the lens of optimism can feel like swimming upstream—like you're going against the current. Everybody at the water cooler wants to have a negative conversation. If you are into that, you can make instant friends. They will let you right in. In fact, they'll suck you in. They'll pull you down. They'll take you the way of the current of our culture.

It is easy to let cynicism or a critical spirit creep into your life without even realizing it. I can speak from experience, because it happened to me a few years ago. I am naturally an optimistic person. I am an Enneagram 7, spontaneous, and a fun-loving extrovert. I have a lot of flaws, but few people would point to me and say, "That guy is a cynic." A few years ago, I had a rare weekend off where I was in town but did not have any Sunday morning responsibilities, so I was excited to take my family to church and participate in the service like a "normal" family.

That morning (go figure), we were running late. Everyone was moving slowly and at their own pace, like we had nowhere to be that morning. Once we finally got into the car, we hit traffic! No one hits Sunday morning traffic. Sunday morning rush hour isn't even a thing, but that day the Pokluda family stopped at every red light between our house and the church building. As I got closer to the church, I thought there had been a massive wreck or pileup, because cars were parked all along the street. What was going on? It turns out it was just a bunch of people going to church. Since we were running later than normal, the odds were stacked against us that we would get in and find a parking spot. But we made it! Things were starting to look up for us.

As we turned into the parking lot, we saw some friends walking in who were members of the "Fifteen Minutes Late Club" like us, but they had already survived the Hunger Games parking lot and found a spot. However, the parking team member led us to the farthest away spot in the farthest away corner of the parking lot. You can imagine my mood at this point.

I was carrying one kid in each arm. Then I realized one didn't have shoes on, so we all trudged back to the car. Then I spilled coffee all over my sleeve. At this point, I'm basically limping across the parking lot covered in children and coffee. On the way I was stopped by someone who wanted to have a pastoral care meeting in the parking lot. I listened as I walked, and prayed for them while dodging cars and juggling kids and coffee. I made it inside the building and checked one child in. Then I made it to the other check-in spot to check the other child in and was told, "Sorry, but you can't. We're full today." I resisted the urge to say, "But I work here." It felt like one of those "There's no room for you in the inn" kind of moments. I realized then that I might not catch a minute of the actual service.

Then I had to meet my in-laws, who were in town visiting us. Looking for two people in a sea of thousands is like a bad game of Where's Waldo?, so I called them on the phone. Obviously they didn't answer the first couple of times, but finally they did. I said, "Where are you guys?" They said, "By the coffee." Hmm. There were at least fifteen different places to get coffee, so I asked for more specifics. Finally I found them, and they said, "Where are we going to sit?" Since I had a kid with me, I needed to go up to the nosebleed seats where we wouldn't be too disruptive, so off we went. But not before I was stopped by a few more people wanting impromptu pastoral care meetings. We eventually made it into the auditorium and sat down.

There was a guest speaker that day. As I settled into my seat, he was just beginning to talk, and I heard him say, "We're going to teach on the prodigal son this morning." I thought, *Come on, now. Could it be any more cliché? I know this story. I've heard it a thousand times. It's the most famous parable ever told. I know my role. I'm the prodigal. I'm the porn guy. I'm the drug guy. I'm the alcohol guy. Check. Check. I grew up in a Christian home. I left. I didn't go to church in college. I came back later on. The prodigal. Check.*

We should have just stayed home.

Then he started talking about the older brother. The older brother was a cynic. He was so consumed with bitterness that he couldn't celebrate the miracle God was doing right in front of him. And God mercifully showed me the drift that had occurred in my heart. I had become a critic, a complainer, a cynic. When did this happen? The guest preacher kept saying, "Come in off the porch!" And I kept thinking, *OK. I will! I'm coming off the porch. I'm sorry!* I was weeping up there in the nosebleeds. That morning God exposed the seed of cynicism that had taken root in my life.

This shift from younger brother to older brother happens in our lives all the time. We come to faith and someone disciples us, is patient with us, cares for us, and shows us the ways of Jesus. Then a little time passes and we look up to see we've become the older brother, completely impatient with immature believers around us, just wondering when they are going to get it together like us.

The Virtue of Optimism

It is oversimplifying the issue to think of optimism as just thinking happier thoughts or trying to put a positive spin on everything that happens. It is so much more than that. Optimism is defined like this: hopefulness and confidence about the future.[1] When we put it like that, we can realize optimism is a basic, fundamental belief of Christianity. Hopefulness, believing the best about the future, and having confidence in what God is doing should be a by-product of our faith in Jesus. When you are optimistic in the midst of obstacles, you can appear foolish. The world might be tempted to think you're naïve or even ignorant. But Christians should see you as faithful.

To put it simply, as Christians, we have read the last chapters of the book and know how this story ends. We know God works all things together for good (Rom. 8:28). We know he wins in the end. So why don't we live like that is true? How did we get so jaded along the way that we've lost sight of one of the foundational realities of the gospel?

The apostle Paul is the biblical template for remaining optimistic in the midst of difficult circumstances. Paul's Christian life was marked by persecution and hardship. Everywhere he went, he was closely watched by the governing authorities because his message about Jesus was viewed as a threat to their power. Ultimately, Paul found himself imprisoned for his role in spreading the gospel—twice.

As he sat in prison, Paul penned a letter to the church at Philippi—a church he helped start and viewed very fondly. At this point, he was most likely chained to a Roman guard twenty-four hours a day. Grab a pen and underline all the optimistic statements you see in this passage:

> Now I want you to know, brothers and sisters, that what has happened to me has actually served to advance the gospel. As a result, it has become clear throughout the whole palace guard and to everyone else that I am in chains for Christ. And because of my chains, most of the brothers and sisters have become confident in the Lord and dare all the more to proclaim the gospel without fear. (Phil. 1:12–14)

Paul looked at his situation—imprisoned, in chains, locked to a guard—and said, "It's OK, because this accomplishes my end goal. My life mission is to advance the gospel. Even me being here, in prison, can do that, so I am content, because what I want most in this world is happening." Let that sink in for a minute. It is one thing to say that from the suburbs but another thing entirely to say it from prison. Paul's letter is saturated with a really convicting hypothesis: "If they're talking about me, they're talking about Jesus."

Paul's life was so intertwined with Jesus Christ that to talk about Paul was to talk about Jesus. Now think about *your* life. If someone is talking about you, are they talking about Christ? Paul was saying here, "Hey, if they're going to talk about me, then that means they get to talk about my Savior, and I'm OK with that. That makes it all worth it."

Then something else happened. He said, in so many words, "The church is being strengthened in the midst of this adversity" (1:12–18). Why? The early church's most influential leader was shackled in prison. How was this a good thing?

Fear is such a powerful motivator. If you're afraid to do something, you can get frozen in fear. But Paul was trying to tell the Philippians to not be deterred by threats of imprisonment. They were afraid to witness because they had been told, "If you share the gospel, we're going to throw you in prison." Paul pointed to himself as an example that, even from prison, God can still use someone to share the gospel.

Optimism in Leadership

My favorite part of my job is not preaching (which I love), writing books, or going to meetings. My favorite part of my job is leading and developing our staff. Everyone may not be the boss, but I believe everyone is a leader—just look behind you, and if anyone is following you, you prove my point. Earlier I mentioned Ken, a supervisor from my corporate days. Let me tell you about another supervisor I had at the same company. Let's call her Kelly.

I worked for Kelly for eighteen months, and I am not sure she ever had a bad day. She was a female Chris Traeger (for all you *Parks & Rec* fans out there), and she exuded joy. Kelly was always composed. She never seemed rattled when something went awry. Even when she had to deliver bad news, she did it in such a way that we all believed her when she said everything was going to be OK. And let me tell you, *everybody* wanted to be on Kelly's team.

A few years ago, *Harvard Business Review* published an article entitled "Primal Leadership: The Hidden Driver of Great Performance," about a study that spent two years researching the importance of attitude and leadership. Here is what they concluded:

> The leader's mood and behaviors drive the moods and behaviors of everyone else. . . . A leader needs to make sure that not only is he [or she] regularly in an optimistic, authentic, high-energy mood, but also that, through [their] chosen actions, [their] followers feel and act that way, too. . . . Emotional leadership is the spark that ignites a company's performance, creating a bonfire of success or a landscape of ashes. Moods matter that much.[2]

Your mood, your attitude, and the lens through which you see the world have a drastic impact on the people around you—particularly if you are a leader. This can be in a workplace, in a small group at your church, or at home with your family. If you lead from a posture of cynicism, morale is going to be low. If you lead from a place of optimism (like Paul), you will see just how contagious it can be, and you will start to see a shift in your followers.

How does that play out practically? Think about your typical day. If it is anything like mine, you bounce from place to place and thing to thing, interacting with different people throughout the day. Each one of my interactions is consequential, be it around the water cooler or with the people at the next table over in the coffee shop. I can be either lost in my thoughts, consumed with my phone, or letting the worries of that particular day impact how I engage with the world around me, *or* I can see each interaction as an opportunity to display the gospel to a lost person who needs to hear it or to remind a fellow believer of the goodness of that message. That is a perspective shift, one we all have to make.

But that is just the workday. My commute is all of four minutes long. Once I get home from work, it has been a long day. Usually I walk straight from my truck to the dinner table, and I'm exhausted. Everything in me wants to have a little "me time." Do you know what I feel like? I feel entitled to check out, but my family is talking about this and that. "You wouldn't believe that so-and-so . . ." "Dad, I made this on my test." "Oh, really? That's good. OK." If I'm not in it at that moment, it impacts the mood of everybody else.

Maybe you've seen the sign, "If Mama ain't happy, ain't nobody happy." Think about how you're leading in your home. Can you remember when your parents argued? Perhaps you were sitting at the kitchen table as your parents fought outside. You sat there wondering if they were going to make it. Tears streamed down your face. You didn't know where this would go. You remember the stressful times, the angst and anxiety they created.

Our attitudes in leadership, particularly in our homes, are far more crucial than many of us realize.

Optimism & Opportunities

Once we grasp the importance of viewing life through the lens of optimism because of the gospel, we then start to see all of the opportunities before us. Paul wasn't just optimistic but also the master of being opportunistic. Here's what he says in Philippians 1:15–18:

> It is true that some preach Christ out of envy and rivalry, but others out of goodwill. The latter do so out of love, knowing that I am put here for the defense of the gospel. The former preach Christ out of selfish ambition, not sincerely, supposing that they can stir up trouble for me while I am in chains. But what does it matter? The important thing is that in every way, whether from false motives or true, Christ is preached. And because of this I rejoice.

Paul saw two kinds of people (but did not break it down into cat people and dog people). One kind preached the gospel for good reasons; one kind preached the gospel for bad reasons.

How does someone preach the gospel out of selfish ambition? What does that mean? Some people read this passage and think, *Ah, he's talking about the prosperity gospel,* and while that may be applicable, I don't think that is his main point here. Paul was talking about people preaching out of a desire to make themselves known or just to create more drama for Paul to have to deal with. And even though they may have made Paul's life more difficult, he found the positive in the situation: the gospel was being preached.

In his letter to the Colossians, Paul wrote, "Be wise in the way you act toward outsiders; make the most of every opportunity" (4:5). He understood the importance of being strategic with each and every opportunity to share the gospel with others.

Paul understood that your unbelieving roommate isn't just somebody to split rent with; they are an opportunity. Your coworker who is far from Jesus isn't just someone to make your nine-to-five more bearable; they are an opportunity. Your children aren't just there to carry on your family name and make sure you're cared for when you're old; they are an opportunity. And when I say "opportunity," I'm not talking about a transactional relationship or a means to an end. I'm saying these are people, with eternal souls, to whom you can tell the Good News about how to live forever. Everyone is an opportunity.

Think about how frustrating it must have been to come against the apostle Paul! It had to be mind-blowingly, pull-out-your-hair aggravating. Think about some of his interactions.

Them: "Hey, we're going to throw him in jail."
Paul: "Hey, man, prison guards need Jesus too. I'll just convert the whole prison."

Them: "We'll beat him."
Paul: "I rejoice in the sufferings of Jesus Christ, the fellowship with him."

Them: "Stone him to death! Drag him outside the city."
Paul: "Ha-ha! You didn't kill me. I'm going back to *this* city."

Them: "OK. We'll chain him up. Chain him to a prison guard."
Paul: "Cool, man. I'll just write the Bible."

Them: "All right. Put his hands in stocks."
Paul: "I'll just dictate to Timothy."

Them: "Kill him!"
Paul: "To die is gain."

Them: "Let him live!"
Paul: "To live is Christ."

Them: "Aaagh! What do we do with this guy?"

Paul understood that this is what the gospel does. It takes any force working against it and just turns it on itself. It's like a fire that, when its opponents think they're going to snuff it out, reveals they are really just pouring kerosene on it—and the gospel is strengthened in those moments.

Can I Not Be Sad?

Right about now you might have a mix of emotions. "Can I not be sad?" It is a fair question. And yes, you can be sad. The point of this chapter is not to try to convince you to never be sad again. Remember the shortest verse in the Bible? Lazarus just died, and it simply says, "Jesus wept" (John 11:35). The one who was about to raise Lazarus from the dead took a moment to grieve with those who grieve, because he saw sin and death in the world that never should have been. It wasn't his first desire.

You can be sad. Just don't stay there, because you know what's waiting for you. You know where this is going. You know where it all leads. Gospel-driven optimism inspires others to share the gospel fearlessly. You lead others well because they can sense the joy and hope inside of you. When you go into a challenge, you come out with a smile. You share the gospel, you lead out of it, and you show others it's always going to be OK. Even if someone responds poorly, they see you're OK. Life is going to go on. You've flipped ahead to the back of the Bible, and you know how the story ends.

THREE QUESTIONS TO ASK YOURSELF

1. How do you struggle with cynicism in your life?

2. Are you more of a glass-half-full or glass-half-empty kind of person? How does that play out in terms of your day-to-day contentment?

3. How can you take a step in growing in optimism today?

CONCLUSION

After Paul goes back and forth, hopelessly asking the question, Why do I do what I don't want to do? in Romans 7, he offers incredible hope at the beginning of chapter 8: "Therefore, there is now no condemnation for those who are in Christ Jesus." "No condemnation" means no judgment. We can escape the consequences of our sin in eternity. That's good news! How do we do it? We repent of our vices and turn to Jesus.

All of my kids have played basketball throughout their elementary school years. As a parent, watching any youth sport when your kids are that age can be a wild ride, but for some reason basketball is even more so. Part of the reason is that at halftime they change goals, so each team must start shooting at the opposite basket.

I remember being at one of Presley's games when she was in fifth grade. After halftime, one of the girls got an offensive rebound but began to dribble toward the other side, to the opponent's goal. Everybody in the stands was shouting, "Hey, you're going the wrong way." Parents. Teammates. The coach. "You're going the wrong way! Turn around! It's *that* way. Go *that* way!" She got almost to half-court, then finally heard and understood. As she was dribbling the ball, she turned and with the same speed, tenacity, and vigor began to move toward the correct goal.

That is the best picture of repentance I can give you. Repenting means turning around when you realize you are running the wrong way. When you find yourself living with a mindset of, *Oh, this world is all there is. I need to stack up dollars. I deserve these things. I need to make a big name for myself. I need to focus on my image and what others think of me. This is what I'm living for.*

If you are a follower of Jesus, the Holy Spirit is saying, *You're going the wrong way! You're going the wrong way! Those are the wrong goals!* Then you can say, "Oh, you're right! I'm going to go *that* way," and with the same speed, tenacity, and vigor, you can begin to move toward Jesus as quickly as you are able.

The aim of this book is not to bring shame or guilt upon you but to show you areas of your life where you may need to repent and turn toward the goals Jesus laid out for us. If you are reading this, and you continue to willfully go back to sin over and over and are not doing everything you can to cut that sin out of your life, you need to be concerned. You need to ask yourself, *Do I really know this Christ?*

Someone who has a relationship with Jesus Christ also has a life marked by repentance. They show a willingness to change and not settle for pet sins. If, like a dog returning to its vomit (Prov. 26:11), you continue in that sin, embracing that sin, cuddling with that sin, saying, "This is just part of who I am. It is what marks me," I am telling you that you need to be concerned. Repentance is turning from that and finding greater satisfaction in Jesus than the things of this world.

If you have never trusted in Christ for the forgiveness of your sins (the very same sins we have discussed in this book), I cannot think of a better time to do so than now. Romans 10:9 makes it really simple for us: "If you declare with your mouth, 'Jesus is Lord,' and believe in your heart that God raised him from the dead, you will be saved." If you have never done that before, repent and turn to Jesus.

Marked by Virtue

Now, if you do have a relationship with Jesus, there should be evidence you can point to that shows it. Your life should produce righteousness. What do I mean by righteousness? The virtues, values, and morality that demonstrate your repentance *because of* what you do and how you live. You live a life marked by the virtues we discussed.

A few years ago, my family and I were on our way to a Christmas party and stopped at a local BBQ place to pick up a couple of sides to bring, because that's how the Pokludas roll. We called ahead, but our order wasn't ready when we arrived, so I started making small talk with the guy behind the counter.

At one point, he said he was blessed. I could tell from his accent that he wasn't from Dallas, so I asked, "Hey, where are you from?" He said, "I'm from Iran." I said, "Oh, man. You said you were blessed. Do you have a faith?" (Side note: that is the question I ask everyone I want to share the gospel with.)

He said, "Yes, I'm of the Islamic faith." "Oh, do you have a mosque you go to in town?" Then he said something very interesting. These are his words, not mine: "No, I don't trust those people."

Now I was just confused.

"What? That's an interesting thing to say. Why not? Who do you trust?"

"I trust Christians. I love Christians."

He said those exact words to me—no hyperbole here. Keep in mind that he had zero idea I'm a pastor. I said, "You trust Christians? Why do you trust Christians?" "Because I came here with four dollars in my pocket. The people who come here, my customers . . . most of them are Christians. They are just so kind to me. I see a kindness that marks them."

Then he took it a step further! He said, "You know something? I know people who have converted to Christianity who have become the most wonderful people. They were terrible people, and then they come into this Christianity, and they are now wonderful people." The Christians in this guy's life had lived out their faith to the point where it was evident their lives were marked by Jesus. Their repentance and righteousness were on full display through the simplest of interactions.

Using Your Story

Think about the life of Paul. He persecuted Christians. He stood idly by as innocent people were killed. He killed innocent people. One day, minding his own business, Paul was walking down the road when Jesus appeared to him and drastically changed his life. After that, he became the greatest missionary and church planter in the New Testament. He was imprisoned, persecuted, and ultimately killed for what he believed. Why would he not back down? He knew exactly what he had seen and experienced. He had to tell everyone.

Throughout the book of Acts, over and over, we see Paul telling his story to anyone who would listen. Even in prison, he gave another message pointing to Christ. He understood the power of his own story of repentance. Anytime he had a captive audience, Paul shared the gospel with people. The Holy Spirit preserved this repetition to show us something.

Paul told his story and pointed to Jesus again and again, and we should too. If you are a Christian, you have been given a key that opened your cage of sin, and as you have been set free, you can go now and tell others about the key that can unlock their cages of bondage to sin. That's what we do! We have been given the task of helping reconcile the rest of the world to God. That means we are the tellers (and re-tellers) of the story of Jesus.

Whatever your story is, you need to use it. The good and the bad, the highs and the lows, the vices and the virtues—everything God has brought you through is to be stewarded by you to point others to him.

I remember sitting in the green room with some coworkers one night and having a conversation with a friend who had walked with Christ faithfully for as long as she could remember. She grew up in a Christian home and never strayed for a day. Now, I'm not saying she never strayed momentarily, but never for an entire day. This woman knew no other life than faithfully walking with Jesus. She had an amazing testimony. I've heard a lot of testimonies, and her story was a rare and beautiful one.

If you have made it this far, you know that is *not* my testimony (sadly). I was feeling feisty that night, so I said, "Convince me that your life has been better than mine. I partied. I got to have sex, I got to do drugs, and I got to indulge in everything the world has to offer. And now you work for someone who works for me. Plus, we both get heaven. Convince me that your life is better than mine."

She didn't hesitate for a second. She just started rattling off the reasons, but two of the things she said stuck out to me the most. She said, "I have had way more fun and I have less scars." *Ouch!* To her credit, she didn't sugarcoat anything. She believed everything she said. And you know what? I do too.

Whatever your story is, God wants to use it to grow his family.

Why would God use any of us? Because people often trust a Christian before they trust Christ (like the friend I made behind the counter at the BBQ restaurant). Very rarely do people just wake up trusting in Christ. More often than not, somebody comes into their life who demonstrates righteousness, repentance, and kindness and tells them about the resurrection of Jesus and how this event two thousand years ago changed their life. First they trust that person, and then they trust that person's God. That is his strategy. That is why he left you here after you trusted Christ and didn't just zap you up into heaven the moment you placed your faith in Jesus. We are *messengers* because we have been given a message.

If you have believed in the message, then you become a messenger. It's my prayer that you will carry it well.

ACKNOWLEDGMENTS

My wife, Monica, works tirelessly at home, taking kids to school and to practice. She wakes up early and stays up late so that the contents of this book can be written, preached, and lived. She is the real hero of our family. If you can only follow one of us, it should be her. She pursues Jesus, prays hard, and studies the Word every day. The fruit of the Spirit bleed from her life more than anyone I've ever known. If only you could know how true that statement is. I'm afraid you'll think it's empty flattery. It's not.

Jon Green's name is not big enough on the front of this book. He continued to push it forward and wrote tirelessly, early and late, after his kids were down. He listened to messages and helped me capture stories I've told along my journey. He let me push back and fight for excellence. He listened, ideated, and partnered with me all while making it fun along the way. His memory is an absolute gift from the Lord. Jon, let's do it again!

I dedicated this book to my mom and dad. I know it's not fun as parents to hear me tell all. You guys were amazing parents—the best! I feel like I grew up on *Little House on the Prairie*. We had breakfasts together around the table every morning. We ate meals at home together—a lost art. My dad gave me a strong work ethic and moral foundation. My mom taught me what it looks like to follow Jesus. I was a punk prodigal who surrendered my life to Jesus later, but they showed me the way early in my life, and I am thankful.

Presley, Finley, and Weston have to be "preacher's kids." They are growing up in the fishbowl of ministry. Please pray the Lord protects them from ever feeling like they need to play the game of Christianity. Please pray their walk with Jesus would be authentic and their faith would be real. I pray that they would find friends to pursue Jesus with in this world where it is popular to do what you want in the flesh. I am grateful for the sacrifices they've made to help Monica and me make much of Jesus.

Carolyn and Jabo Rubin have helped shaped that woman at the top who has been the greatest gift to me aside from Jesus. They help with the kids while we travel the world preaching, teaching, and writing. They provided a second home to me early in my journey and have been the best in-laws anyone could ask for.

So much of what is in this book I learned from Todd Wagner. He led me into a relationship with Jesus and modeled leadership for me during my time at Watermark. I will be eternally grateful for the wisdom he shared and especially for the truth of the gospel that dripped from every sermon he preached. He and Alex are incredible parents, and Monica and I consider it a gift to have gotten to learn from them.

Jennie and Zac Allen have been great friends and cheerleaders to me. Jennie is the big sister I don't deserve. She has been an inspiration to much of the ministry I do, and Zac always shows up at the right time to tell me the truth when I need to hear it. Before I ever wrote a book, they were there telling me I should. We all need friends like them to push us to be more of who God desires us to be.

My agent, Don Gates, is a champion of this work. He has kept me on track and moving forward. The team at Baker Books have been great to work with, and they have made this work possible. I am thankful! Dr. Michael Chapman and Dr. Grant Beckham have been there to help keep me healthy and thinking clearly. When the chairs fell, they helped me pick the right ones back up.

The members of Harris Creek have been so supportive of having a pastor who writes and speaks elsewhere. I am thankful for the grace they show me and for allowing me to develop other communicators. The staff at Harris Creek have also been so supportive through the past four years. I work with some of the best ministers of the gospel on the planet, and I am grateful for the way they serve Jesus's church.

NOTES

Introduction

1. Eugene Peterson, *A Long Obedience in the Same Direction* (Downers Grove, IL: InterVarsity, 2019), 10.

Part 1 The Ancient Battles

1. Becky Little, "How the Seven Deadly Sins Began as 'Eight Evil Thoughts,'" History, March 25, 2021, https://www.history.com/news/seven-deadly-sins-origins.

Chapter 1 Pride & Humility

1. C. S. Lewis, *Mere Christianity* (New York: HarperCollins, 2001), 122. Copyright © 1942, 1943, 1944, 1952 by CS Lewis Pte Ltd. Used by permission.

Chapter 3 Greed & Generosity

1. Alexandria White, "73% of Americans Rank Their Finances as the No. 1 Stress in Life, according to New Capital One CreditWise Survey," CNBC, July 20, 2021, https://www.cnbc.com/select/73-percent-of-americans-rank-finances-as-the-number-one-stress-in-life.

2. TMZ Sports, "Floyd Mayweather Drops $1 Million on Cars for His Inner Circle, Rolls-Royce for Himself," TMZ, June 6, 2021, https://www.tmz.com/2021/06/06/floyd-mayweather-drops-1-million-on-cars-for-his-inner-circle/.

3. Alison Millington and Business Insider, "The First Thing 14 Lottery Winners Have Bought after Finding Out They Were Rich," *Insider*, January 29, 2020, https://www.businessinsider.com/how-lottery-winners-spend-winnings-2016-1.

Chapter 4 Apathy & Diligence

1. Aaron Earls, "Apathy in Churches Looms Large for Pastors," Lifeway Research, May 10, 2022, https://research.lifeway.com/2022/05/10/apathy-in-churches-looms-large-for-pastors/.

2. D. A. Carson, *For the Love of God: A Daily Companion for Discovering the Riches of God's Word*, vol. 2 (Wheaton: Crossway, 1999), 49.

Chapter 5 Lust & Self-Control

1. *Merriam-Webster Dictionary*, s.v. "lust," accessed June 21, 2022, https://www.merriam-webster.com/dictionary/lust.

2. Ralph Waldo Emerson, "Spiritual Laws," in *Essays: First Series*, Emerson Central, accessed June 21, 2022, https://emersoncentral.com/texts/essays-first-series/spiritual-laws/.

3. X3, "Sex and Glue," XXX Church, November 30, 2014, https://xxxchurch.com/men/sex-glue.html.

4. "Fast Facts about Pornography," Fight the New Drug, accessed July 21, 2022, https://fightthenewdrug.org/fast-facts/.

Chapter 8 Busyness & Rest

1. Andy Crouch @ahc, "Also, if I've ever said no to you," Twitter post, June 30, 2021, https://twitter.com/ahc/status/1410272197084598273.

2. James Gilchrist Lawson, ed., "Prayer," *Cyclopedia of Religious Anecdotes* (New York: Fleming H. Revell, 1923), 303.

Chapter 10 Cynicism & Optimism

1. *Lexico*, s.v. "optimist," accessed June 21, 2022, https://www.lexico.com/definition/optimist.

2. Daniel Goleman, Richard E. Boyatzis, and Annie McKee, "Primal Leadership: The Hidden Driver of Great Performance," *Harvard Business Review* (December 2001), https://hbr.org/2001/12/primal-leadership-the-hidden-driver-of-great-performance.

ABOUT THE AUTHORS

Jonathan "JP" Pokluda is the lead pastor of a church in Waco, Texas, called Harris Creek. For over a decade he led the largest Christian singles gathering in America, The Porch. He's had a front-row seat watching thousands of relationships form and flourish while others fizzled out. JP's most recent book, *Outdated*, was written after years of observing the changing landscape of dating. He didn't come to understand the grace of the gospel until his early twenties, after being involved in different denominational churches his entire life. This ignited a desire in him to inspire young adults to radically follow Jesus Christ and unleash them to change the world. His bestselling book *Welcome to Adulting* offers Millennials a road map to navigating faith, finding a spouse, managing finances, and preparing for the future. JP's partner in ministry is Monica, his wife of sixteen years, and together they disciple their children Presley, Finley, and Weston.

Jon Green has been on staff at Harris Creek since 2013. He is a graduate of Baylor University and is the managing editor of BibleReadingPlan.org, a daily devotional and Bible study. Jon and his wife, Amanda, live in Waco, Texas, and have three young children: Micah, Elsie, and Bennett.

—————— CONNECT WITH JP ——————

 Jonathan Pokluda | @JPokluda | @JPokluda

Friend, I pray that this resource fills your heart with hope and contentment and offers you clear direction for living a virtue-filled life in the twenty-first century. I write books because I want to see people follow God and live out his calling on their lives. I don't invest a lot of money in marketing. I simply try to write truths that are helpful to you. With that said, YOU are my very best advertising. Would you take a picture of yourself with the book and share it? If you tag @jpokluda, I will re-share your post. Thank you for your prayers and support! I know God has a plan for you, I know his plan is good, and I know his Word will never lead us astray. I pray you read it in and live it out.

Much love!

JP

YOU'RE AN ADULT . . .
NOW WHAT?

Adulting is hard. But sometimes we make it harder than it has to be. If you're struggling to find a footing in the world of adult life, these witty, non-patronizing guides are for you.

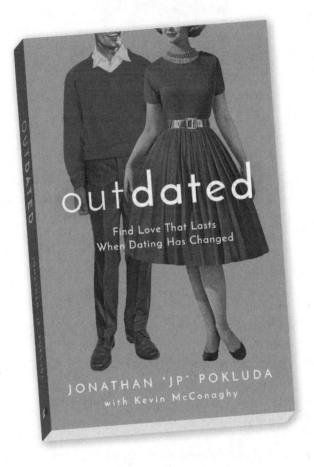

- Become a **#WhyDoIBook** ambassador by taking a photo of yourself with the book and sharing it on your social media platforms.

- Write a book review on your blog or on a retailer site.

- Pick up a copy for friends, family, or anyone who you think would enjoy and be challenged by its message!

- Share this message on Twitter, Facebook, or Instagram:
  I loved #WhyDoIDoWhatIDontWantToDo and #WhyDoIBook by @JPokluda // @ReadBakerBooks

- Recommend this book for your church, workplace, book club, or class.

- Follow Baker Books on social media and tell us what you like.

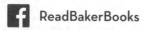 **ReadBakerBooks**

ReadBakerBooks

 **ReadBakerBooks**